THE ATLAS OF THE
BIBLE
LANDS

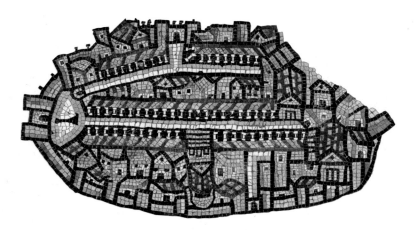

This edition published by
Macdonald Young Books,
an imprint of Wayland Publishers Ltd
61 Western Road
Hove, East Sussex BN3 1JD

You can find
Macdonald Young Books
on the internet at
http://www.myb.co.uk

ISBN 0 7500 2633 2

A catalogue record for this book
is available from the British Library

The Atlas of the Bible Lands
was created and produced by McRae Books,
via de' Rustici, 5 – Florence (Italy)

Text Andrea Dué
Main illustrations Paola Ravaglia, Matteo Chesi,
Gian Paolo Faleschini, Federico Micheli,
Antonella Pastorelli, Ivan Stalio
Other illustrations Alessandro Cantucci, Lorenzo
Cecchi, Ferruccio Cucchiarini, Valentina Di Serio,
Michela Gaudenzi, Paola Holguín, Federico Micheli,
Andrea Morandi
Editorial consultant Sandro Servi
Translation Anne McRae
Graphic Design Marco Nardi
Maps and cutouts Adriano Nardi, Ornella Fassio
Colour separations R.A.F., Florence (Italy)

Printed in Italy by Giunti Industrie Grafiche, Prato

THE ATLAS OF THE
BIBLE LANDS

People, Daily Life and Traditions

Text by Andrea Dué

Illustrations by Paola Ravaglia, Matteo Chesi,
Gian Paolo Faleschini, Federico Micheli,
Antonella Pastorelli, Ivan Stalio

Macdonald Young Books

Palaeolithic (Old Stone Age) 700,000–15,000 BC
Mesolithic (Middle Stone Age) 15,000–8000 BC
Neolithic (New Stone Age) 8000–4500 BC
Chalcolithic 4,500–3300 BC
Bronze Age: Early 3300–2000 BC, Middle 2000–1550 BC, Late 1550–1200 BC
Iron Age 1200–586 BC
Babylonian and Persian Period 586–332 BC
Hellenistic Period 332–37 BC
Roman Period 37 BC–AD 324
Byzantine Period AD 324–640
Early Arab Period AD 640–1099
Crusader Period AD 1099–1291
Mameluke and Ottoman Period AD 1291–1917
British Mandate 1917–1948
State of Israel 1948–

This exquisitely moulded gold figure dates to about the 16th century BC. It was found at Gezer in ancient Canaan and probably shows a Canaanite goddess.

This early Christian fresco shows heretics who refuse to listen to the Word of the new Christian God.

The Good Shepherd is a common symbol in Christianity. The shepherd represents Jesus, and the lamb one of the flock of believers he cares for. The motif predates Christian times.

The Damascus gate in Jerusalem. The beautiful Gate was built during the rule of the Islamic leader Suleyman the Magnificent.

Contents

Introduction

Ivory plaque showing people with prisoners making offerings to a ruler. From the rich hoard of ivories dating to the Late Bronze Age found in the fortress town of Megiddo. It was probably a decoration from a piece of furniture.

Saint Agnes, from a 4th century fresco in a catacomb near Rome, Italy.

The *Atlas of the Bible Lands* charts the history of a large part of the Middle East, from prehistory to the present day. It focuses on the tiny piece of land in the eastern Mediterranean now occupied by the states of Israel, Jordan, Lebanon and Syria. But because events in biblical history involved all the great powers of the time, from Egypt to Greece to Mesopotamia, the Atlas also deals with these regions.

Over the centuries the Middle East has witnessed the rise and fall of many peoples and civilizations. In ancient times, the Holy Land was home to a people whom we now refer to as the Canaanites, and the land was called Canaan. Since then it has been known variously as the Promised Land, the Kingdom of Israel, Judah, Judaea, Palestine and Israel. As the focal point of three world religions – Judaism, Christianity and Islam – it has always aroused curiousity, and provoked strong feelings. Wars have been fought to control it and thousands of people have died (many of them foreigners) to defend it. This Atlas introduces the kaleidoscope of events and people in the lands where the Bible was first written down.

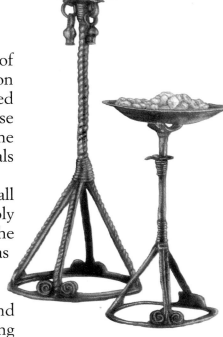

Incense burners from Canaan, dating to the time before the Israelites settled there.

Overland trade in the Bible Lands was carried out by caravans of camels. The main trade routes were dotted with bustling caravanseries, where merchants and their animals could eat and rest from their journey. Water was available at these stopover points but food had to be carried together with the goods.

Before the Bible

The Bible Lands were inhabited from earliest times by peoples of many different cultures. Some of the oldest remains of modern human beings, who lived over 100,000 years ago, have been found in Palestine. The peoples of the Bible Lands were among the first in the world to develop agriculture. Gradually, beginning from about 9000 BC, people began to grow crops rather than simply gathering wild cereals. They began to keep animals, firstly sheep and goats, then cattle and pigs. The beginning of agriculture is known as the Neolithic revolution. It greatly changed the way many people lived. The population increased; villages grew in number, size and power. Tools, ornaments and pottery were produced in larger quantities for home use and trade. However, these changes did not affect everyone in the area equally. Hunters and gatherers and nomadic herders still lived alongside more complex communities in farming villages and walled cities.

Crossroads of prehistory
In ancient times the Levant was a land bridge between the great civilizations of Mesopotamia and Egypt, and also between Europe and Asia. Even earlier, groups of *homo erectus*, (the ancestors of modern humans), passed through the region as they moved from Africa to populate the rest of the world. The handaxe (above) from Ubeidiya (one of the oldest archaeological sites outside of Africa), near the Sea of Galilee, dates from 1.5 million years ago, the age of *homo erectus*.

Palaeolithic, Mesolithic and Neolithic
These are the terms archaeologists use to divide the era known as the Stone Age, during which people used stone to make tools. See the chart on p. 6 for approximate dates.

Natufian culture
People of the Natufian culture, who lived in the Middle Stone Age, were the first in the Levant to live in small villages. They lived by hunting, and by gathering the wild cereals that grew freely in the region. Their way of life was an important step in the move towards farming. They gradually began to gather food in a more organized way, making use of tools, like the sickle. They also began to store a part of what they had gathered.

The earliest inhabitants of the Levant were hunters and gatherers. This Palaeolithic rock painting shows people hunting gazelle, which were common prey at that time. It comes from a sanctuary on Mount Karkom in the Negev Desert.

People of the Natufian culture were among the first to make extensive use of jewellery. They used a variety of materials, including bone, stone, shell and eggs. The fish-shaped pendant (top left) and the necklace (above) are two fine examples. The gazelle-shaped sickle handle (right) has been skilfully carved from bone.

During the Neolithic period it was common practice in Jericho to separate the skull from the skeleton. Sometimes the skulls had faces modelled in plaster. They were probably used for ancestor worship.

The invention of pottery
Pottery was first made in the Levant around 6000 BC. Although pottery vessels break, the material itself is incredibly strong. Archaeologists use pieces of pottery to find out when people of different cultures lived and to learn how they developed.

The birth of agriculture
Agriculture in the Middle East began in the Fertile Crescent (a wide arc stretching from Mesopotamia through Palestine and down to the Nile Valley in Egypt). People began to sow seeds to raise crops rather than relying on wild cereals. The first traces of this type of cultivation date from around 9000 BC. Soon afterwards goats and sheep were domesticated and raised for the milk, meat and wool they produced.

Dogs were probably the first animals to be tamed. At a burial site in Palestine a child with its arms around a puppy (probably a wolf cub) was found. Dating from about 9000 BC, it suggests that dogs had been domesticated by that date.

The tiny pottery statue (left) dates from around 5000 BC. It is one of the most beautiful of the many statues of women that have been found in the Middle East. They all show the Mother Goddess, a fertility goddess worshipped by many early farming peoples. The figure's female attributes are strongly emphasized.

Tiny figures like this one (left), made of plaster over a reed base, have been found at Ain Ghazel in Jordan. Dating from about 6800 BC, we do not know whether they represent ancestors or gods, but they almost certainly had some kind of sacred or religious meaning.

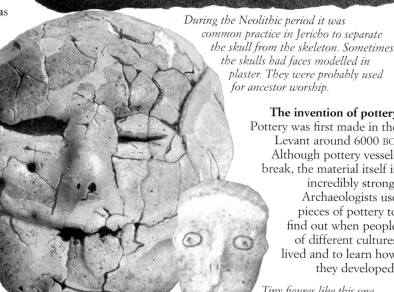

Metalworkers – the Chalcolithic and Bronze Ages

A great leap forward took place in the Levant from about 4500 BC when people began to use metal to make tools. During the Chalcolithic period (from the Greek word *chalcos* for copper), there was a great increase in the number of settlements. The classic pattern of Mediterranean agriculture was already established: farmers grew cereals, pulses, olives and dates and raised sheep, goats, cattle, pigs and some deer. From about 3000 BC the inhabitants of the Levant began to use bronze in their tool-making. During the Bronze Age larger walled cities became widespread.

A breathtaking hoard of copper objects from the Chalcolithic period was found in 1961 in the Judean Desert, including the two pieces shown here. The technical quality of the tools and vessels, made using a lost wax technique, is astounding even by modern standards.

Salt formations like this one occur naturally on the shores of the Dead Sea.

The Dead Sea

The Dead Sea is a lake lying between Israel and Jordan. At 400 metres below sea level, it is the lowest body of water on earth. In Hebrew it is known as the Salt Sea, because of its very high salt content. No animals or plants can survive in its waters. The Dead Sea was an important source of salt and bitumen in ancient times. Salt was traded far and wide. Bitumen, which occurs naturally in the Dead Sea, was used to make glue.

Ossuary from about 3500 BC, found in Jaffa. Ossuaries often take the form of houses or stylized animals.

Burial customs

People began to care about the way they buried their dead sometime in the Middle Palaeolithic period (80,000–35,000 BC). This is seen as a major step in human development because it means that people probably believed in some kind of life after death. Natufian burials have been found containing bodies on their sides in a crouched position. Some have jewellery and other goods buried with them. By Chalcolithic times it may have been common to bury people twice. Once the flesh had rotted the bones were put in special clay chests, called ossuaries.

The invention of writing

Early forms of writing were invented about 3100 BC. The first written documents were lists of agricultural products and records of trade. People soon realized the power of the written word and began to record their history, myths and religious beliefs.

Cuneiform tablet from Mesopotamia with details of the amount of barley needed to make beer, malt and other products.

The growth of cities

Towards the end of the Chalcolithic period many villages were abandoned, perhaps because of famine or drought, or attack by invaders. After 3300 BC, during the Early Bronze Age, new towns sprang up, many on new sites. Over the centuries cities became a significant feature of life in Canaan. They were in a good position for trading with wealthy societies in Mesopotamia and Egypt. Cities in Canaan flourished for several hundred years until they began to decline around 2300 BC.

Jericho

The city of Jericho, just north of the Dead Sea, was one of the earliest cities in the world. By early Neolithic times, it already had a complex defence system, made up of a ditch and a stone wall 3 metres thick. Inside the walls stood a huge tower, 9 metres tall with a staircase inside (probably a watch-tower). There were warehouses, water reservoirs, buildings for worship and comfortable houses. An astonishing amount of technology, social organization and wealth were required to build the city. Jericho probably became rich by trading the salt, bitumen and sulphur on the shores of the Dead Sea. By 8000 BC the city probably had about 2,000 inhabitants – not large by modern standards, but a huge settlement in those times.

Map labels

Baisamoun
Achzib
Naveh Yam
SEA OF GALILEE
Ubeidiya
Tel 'All
Megiddo
Beth Shean
Hadera
Shechem
PALESTINE
Tel Aviv
Azor
Ein Ghazel
River Jordan
Lod
Gezer
Jericho
Teleilat el-Ghassul
Ashdod
Jerusalem
DEAD SEA
Judaean Desert
En-gedi

The large map on this page shows some of the settlements in Palestine during the Chalcolithic period, as well as one or two from earlier times.

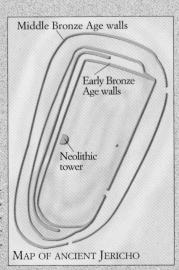

Middle Bronze Age walls
Early Bronze Age walls
Neolithic tower

MAP OF ANCIENT JERICHO

Trade

The map shows the main trade routes (red lines) and centres of trade. Towns like Aleppo, Mari and Haran in the northern Levant, were important market-places. They imported raw materials, such as wood and precious metals from Anatolia and traded them east to Mesopotamia and south to Egypt. In return, they received items like copper, gold, silver, tin and lapis lazuli from Mesopotamia, which they moved west to the Mediterranean. Egypt sent gold, alabaster, copper and diorite (a kind of rock) north. The city states in the region stayed in contact to make sure that the trade routes remained open. Controlling trade was lucrative and there were frequent wars among the larger cities to gain control over international routes.

When diplomatic means failed, city states often turned to war. This 18th century BC clay model of a four-wheeled war chariot comes from northern Syria. The four-wheeled chariot pulled by asses was replaced by the faster two-wheeled, horse-drawn one sometime after the 18th-century BC.

The Age of the Patriarchs

In the Bible the patriarchs are Abraham, Isaac and Jacob. Jacob's sons, including Joseph, were the ancestors of the twelve tribes of Israel. The first patriarch, Abraham, left the city of Ur in southern Mesopotamia and journeyed to Canaan and Egypt. Isaac and Jacob also travelled widely between Canaan, Egypt and Mesopotamia. Joseph and his brothers settled in Egypt. According to the Bible, these men are the forefathers of the nation of Israel. It is hard to prove if they ever existed and scholars have very different opinions about if, and when, they lived. Recent archaeological evidence largely coincides with the world described in the Bible, although it doesn't provide any proof that the patriarchs existed as real men. Most scholars think that the patriarchal stories are set in about 2000–1750 BC. Many large and powerful cities flourished in the Middle East at that time, particularly in Mesopotamia and Egypt. The cities were linked by international trade routes. Traders kept lists of imports and from these we know that gold, silver, copper, tin, oil, wine and spices were among the items traded. Canaan was inhabited by a Semitic people, probably Amorites. There was a gradual rebirth of towns and trade in Canaan in the patriarchal age, probably stimulated by contact with Mesopotamia and Egypt.

● H*

● Aleppo

● Ugarit

● Byblos

This strange, staring human face is a pottery vase from Jericho, made in the Middle Bronze Age (17th century BC). Very few pieces of pottery of this type have been found dating from the same period.

Canaan in the age of the patriarchs

Several quite large cities developed in Canaan during the Middle Bronze Age, particularly along the coast and the valleys leading inland from the sea. Hazor, near Galilee, became an important city. It covered 80 hectares and probably had about 20,000 inhabitants. Canaan had strong links with Mesopotamia and Egypt, but it also had a distinctive culture of its own. The Canaanites produced particularly fine metalwork, jewellery and ivory carvings.

Egypt

The Middle Kingdom in ancient Egypt (about 2040–1750 BC) was a period of stability. Egypt was united with its capital at Thebes. Trading links were rebuilt with other countries. From the 19th century BC onwards many Canaanites settled in Egypt.

Abraham's journey from Ur to Canaan

The thick line on the map shows the route that Abraham's father, Terah, may have taken from Ur to Haran in the north. The city of Haran lay at a strategic point on international trade routes. According to the Bible, God ordered Abraham to leave Haran and travel to Canaan and then south into Egypt. 'Now the Lord said to Abraham, "Go from your country and your kindred and your father's house to the land I will show you and I shall make you a great nation...". Abraham was seventy-five years old when he departed from Haran. And Abraham took Sara his wife, and Lot his brother's son, and all their possessions which they had gathered.' Genesis, 12, 3–5

Palace cities of the Middle East

Ebla and Mari in Syria are two of the largest palace cities known. They were at their height between 2400 and 1750 BC. Both cities had a huge central palace surrounded by private housing. The palace at Mari had 300 rooms and covered 2.5 hectares. The city itself was surrounded by a thick wall 20 metres high enclosing an area of about 100 hectares. Archaeologists have found more than 24,000 clay tablets at Mari. They contain records of trade, taxes, tolls on the Euphrates River, legal and political matters, and even how to retrieve runaway slaves and interpret dreams. They have provided scholars with a wealth of information about life at the time.

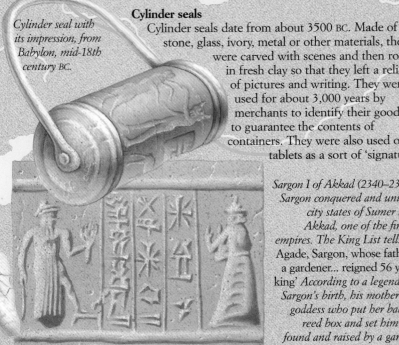

Cylinder seal with its impression, from Babylon, mid-18th century BC.

Cylinder seals

Cylinder seals date from about 3500 BC. Made of stone, glass, ivory, metal or other materials, they were carved with scenes and then rolled in fresh clay so that they left a relief of pictures and writing. They were used for about 3,000 years by merchants to identify their goods and to guarantee the contents of containers. They were also used on tablets as a sort of 'signature'.

Sargon I of Akkad (2340–2315 BC). Sargon conquered and united the city states of Sumer to form Akkad, one of the first great empires. The King List tells us 'In Agade, Sargon, whose father was a gardener... reigned 56 years as king.' According to a legend about Sargon's birth, his mother was a goddess who put her baby in a reed box and set him adrift on a river. He was found and raised by a gardener's family. This story is similar to the one about Moses.

The Hammurabi stela, made of black stone, stands over two metres tall. The scene at the top shows the god Shamash giving the laws to Hammurabi.

Ziggurats

The cities of Mesopotamia were all dedicated to a god or goddess, who was believed to reside in the city. Many cities placed the divinity's temple on the top of several tall platforms. These platform structures are called ziggurats. The earliest ziggurats date from about 5000 BC. The ziggurat at Ur (below) dates from about 3,000 years later. The ziggurat at Babylon, dedicated to the god Marduk, is probably the basis for the biblical story of the Tower of Babel.

Zimri-Lim (about 1775–1760 BC) was King of the Syrian palace city of Mari. He was overthrown by King Hammurabi of Babylon.

● **Mari**

The Sumerian King List

Sometime around 2000 BC a scribe made a list of all the kings of Sumer from earliest times. It begins: *'When kingship was lowered from heaven, kingship was first in Eridu...'*. The King List also refers to a great flood, like the one in the Bible. *'After the Flood had swept over the earth and when kingship was lowered again from heaven, kingship was first in Kish...'*.

Several copies of the King List have survived. It appears to be a mixture of fact and fiction. The aim of the list was to show that at every age one city was more powerful than all the others.

An ancient law code

Hammurabi was King of Babylon from 1792–50 BC. The stela associated with his name is one of the most important documents we have on life and society in patriarchal times. Written in Akkadian, it lists about 280 legal decisions made by the King on questions ranging from trade, tariffs, marriage, divorce, assault, theft, slavery and debt. Many of the laws are similar in content and wording to the ones that the Hebrew prophet Moses would later record. For example, it contains the idea of *'an eye for an eye, and a tooth for a tooth'*.

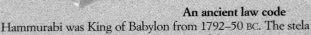

Tigris river

● **Babylon**

Euphrates river

Uruk ●

Mesopotamia

The first farming villages appeared on the flatlands between the Tigris and Euphrates Rivers in about 6000 BC. This area is known as Mesopotamia (meaning 'between the rivers'). It is now part of Iraq. The early farmers used irrigation to water the fertile plains; they produced more food so that the population grew and excess produce could be traded. By about 3500 BC, the first cities had appeared in the south, in an area called Sumer. Ur, the city from which Abraham's family may have come, was one of the largest Sumerian cities. Over the centuries other city-states developed to the north and west. Between about 2500–1500 BC they fought many wars to gain power and control trade routes.

Ur ●

Ancient texts say that Ur was on the sea. The coastline was much closer to the city than it is today. The lighter colour shows the shoreline in patriarchal times. Ur was sacked by an invading army in about 2000 BC. It was rebuilt and continued to flourish. Some scholars think that Abraham's family may have left Ur to escape this attack.

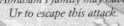

Plants and Animals of the Bible Lands

The Bible Lands cover the area we now call the Middle East, from Egypt to the Persian Gulf and from Turkey to Arabia. The Levant, consisting of the modern countries of Lebanon, Syria, Israel and Jordan, was the central region of the Bible Lands. The geography of this huge area is varied and includes high mountains and deserts, as well as fertile river valleys and coastal strips. The climate is generally hot and dry in summer, with cool to cold winters. Water is the most valuable resource in the region. Rainfall is changeable and in many areas groundwater is scarce. Ancient farmers and herders often had to move because land that would support crops or feed animals one year was no longer fertile the next. Many crops were grown, including wheat, barley, grapes, figs, olives, pomegranates and dates. Sheep, goats, and cattle were kept for milk, wool, leather and meat. Donkeys, camels and horses were used for transport. There were many wild animals as well, some of which, like the lion, have since become extinct in the area.

Black figs. Fresh and dried figs and dates were wholesome foods.

Olives were a staple crop. The fruit was eaten, and could also be made into oil for cooking and lighting.

Farmers grew native species of wheat and barley. They used them to make bread and to brew beer.

Pomegranates have fleshy, juicy seeds and were a prized fruit in ancient times. They often appear in texts and images as symbols of fertility.

Walnut tree.

Cyprus trees.

Cedar tree. Cedar wood is light, soft and strong. It was a precious wood, used for decoration and furniture.

Olive tree.

Fig tree.

Almonds were a favourite food. They were also used to make a valuable oil.

Almond tree.

A land of milk and honey
The following description of Canaan is given in the Bible: *'For the Lord thy God bringeth thee into a good land, a land of brooks of water, of fountains and depths that spring out of valleys and hills; a land of wheat and barley, and vines, and fig trees, and pomegranates; a land of olive oil, and honey'.* (Deuteronomy 8, 8).

The olive
The olive tree is native to the Levant. In biblical times olive oil became an important resource. It was used not only to flavour and cook food, but also for lighting, in medicine, in religious ceremonies, and as a base for perfumes. It was exported far and wide.

Grapes and wine-making
Grapes were enjoyed as a refreshing late-summer fruit. They were also dried as raisins and could be eaten throughout the year. Wine-making was a common activity and Palestine became famous for the quality of its wines.

Bunches of black and white grapes were harvested in late summer for food and wine.

Beasts of burden
Donkeys and mules were the most common pack animals. They were widely used by rich and poor alike for transport and to carry heavy loads. The one-humped, Arabian camel also became an important beast of burden, although it was probably only domesticated in about 1000 BC. Horses were only kept by the rich. They were symbols of power and prestige and were mainly used for war.

Sugar and spice

Honey was the main sweetener for foods. Initially it was taken from wild bees; in later times bees were kept specially. Salt was used for cooking and to preserve foods. Both local and imported herbs and spices were used to flavour dishes.

Animals, like this winged bull from the city of Susa in ancient Persia, were often used as decorative elements.

Animals as symbols

Animals were commonly used as religious symbols. In some places animals were worshiped as divine beings or as images of gods. For example, the gods of ancient Egypt were often represented by animal heads.

A golden calf, used as a cult figure. In the Bible, Moses smashes a figure like this because the Hebrews are forbidden to worship idols.

Early inhabitants of the Bible Lands left many rock paintings. The majority of these images show animals or scenes with men hunting animals.

Animals and religion

Many animals had a special meaning or position in the religions of the Bible Lands. For example, on the Day of Atonement, Hebrew priests released a goat into the wilderness as a sign that people's sins had been taken away.

The medieval illustration below shows the creation of the animals. The animals can be identified as an elephant, a hare, a cat, a porcupine, a lion, a dog, a sheep, an antelope, a bull, a horse and a deer.

Wild ibex still live in some areas of modern Israel and Palestine.

Wild animals

Many of the wild animals mentioned in the Bible no longer exist in the Levant. They have been wiped out by extensive hunting. Lions and tigers have disappeared from the entire region, while hippopotamuses, crocodiles, bears and ostriches still survive in some areas.

Fishing

Fishing was widely practised along the coastlines and in the inland rivers and lakes. The fish in the Sea of Galilee were an important source of food for the people of Canaan.

Domestic animals

Sheep and goats were kept from very early times. Nomadic herders relied on them for milk, cheese, meat and clothing. Shepherds guarded the flocks day and night to protect them from wild animals. Cattle were kept for milk, meat and leather. Poultry and other birds were kept too. Farmers used oxen and donkeys to draw ploughs, wagons and carts.

The arid conditions of much of the region make it an ideal home for snakes. The snake became a potent symbol of evil in the Bible.

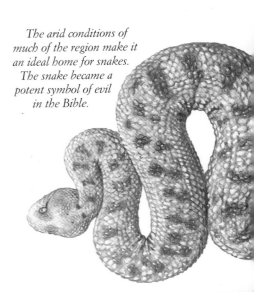

Nations and Peoples

The Middle East was inhabited by a vast, everchanging mosaic of peoples in biblical times. Ancient Egypt and the successive civilizations of Mesopotamia – Sumeria, Akkadia, Old Babylonia, Assyria, New Babylonia and Persia – all greatly influenced Palestine, either by conquering it or through trade and the exchange of ideas. In 333 BC, the Persians were ousted by Alexander the Great who introduced Greek civilization, which was, in turn, overrun by the Romans. Many other nations are mentioned in the Bible, including the Hittites, Philistines, Phoenicians, Edomites, Moabites and many, many more. To a greater or lesser extent, they all left their mark on Palestine, influencing the customs and religion of the Hebrews and, later, the Christians.

The Hittites
The Hittites were an Indo-European people who originally came from southern Russia. They controlled Syria and the lands north of Canaan for many centuries. The Hittites fought against Egypt for control of the Levant. Their empire disappeared just before the Israelites settled in Cannan, probably destroyed by the invading Sea Peoples (see pp. 22–23).

The Hurrians and other peoples of Anatolia and the north
The Hurrians migrated into northern Mesopotamia from the mountains of Armenia. One group, the Mitanni, established an empire in Mesopotamia. When the Hittite and Hurrian empires declined, other small kingdoms appeared, including the Carians, Lydians and Phrygians. The Urartians occupied the area of Mount Ararat, where Noah's Ark is said to have come to rest after the flood.

The Greeks move east
When Classical Greece declined in the 4th century BC, it was conquered by Alexander the Great, King of the tiny kingdom of Macedonia in northern Greece. Alexander went on to conquer a huge empire, encompassing the whole of the Bible Lands.

Tiny gold statue of a Hittite king or god, from the 14th century BC.

Romans

BLACK SEA

Greeks

Lydians

Phrygians

Carians

Cretans

Scythians

Urartians

Hittites

Hurrians

MEDITERRANEAN SEA

Cypriotes

Phoenicians

Aramaeans

Assyrians

Canaanites

Israelites

Philistines

Ammonites

Moabites

Edomites

Babylonians

Chaldaeans

The pyramids

Egyptians

Midianites

Dedanites

Sumerians

Persians

Alexander the Great with his favourite horse, Bucephalus.

Gold coin from Ancient Persia showing the great warrior king, Darius.

Ancient Egypt
The powerful Egyptian civilization existed throughout biblical times. It played an important role in the history of the Middle East for 3,000 years and is mentioned often in the Bible (see pp. 18–19).

The Canaanites
Canaan covered more or less the same area that the modern states of Israel, Syria and Lebanon occupy today. It was inhabited by peoples organized in small city-states (listed in the Bible as Hittites, Girgashites, Amorites, Canaanites, Perizzites, Hivites and Jebusites) who are known collectively as Canaanites. There were frequent wars among the various groups. Many Canaanites were farming peoples, while others were craftspeople and traders. The Israelites settled in the heart of Canaan and gradually conquered the other people there (see pp. 22–23).

A Canaanite water flask from the 13th century BC.

Statue of the Canaanite god, Baal.

Ancient Persia
Under Cyrus the Great the ancient Persians conquered Babylon and established a large empire that lasted for over 200 years. The Persians were tolerant of different customs and religions among the peoples in their empire. They allowed the exiled Jews in Babylon to return to Israel. The Persian empire was destroyed by Alexander the Great in 333 BC (see pp. 36–37).

Mesopotamia

The area between the Tigris and Euphrates Rivers, known as Mesopotamia, was occupied by several powerful civilizations throughout the biblical period. After the early Sumerian and Akkadian peoples, the Amorites took power in about 2000 BC, establishing the first Babylonian empire (see pp. 10–11). The Amorites were a desert people of Semitic origin. Their empire was destroyed in about 1500 BC by the Hittites. The Assyrians (see pp. 26–27) established an empire in Mesopotamia from the 9th century BC. This was followed by the second Babylonian empire (see pp. 32–33) which ended during the 6th century BC when the Persian king, Cyrus, conquered Babylon.

This bronze statue dating from the 18th century BC was found at Larsa in modern Iraq. It is thought to show King Hammurabi (see pp. 10–11) as he kneels in prayer to an Amorite god.

The Cypriotes

The Mediterranean island of Cyprus (ancient Alashiya) had close trading and cultural links with the Levant. It was a major source of copper in the ancient world.

This 12th century BC bronze statue found on Cyprus shows a god sitting on a throne.

This building was the Treasury in the beautiful rock-cut city of Petra, in modern Jordan. It was the capital of the Nabataean kingdom.

Arab peoples

The Arabian peninsula was inhabited by various peoples, most of whom were nomadic herders. The groups mentioned in the Bible include the Midianites and the Nabataeans.

The biblical view

'The sons of Noah who went forth from the Ark were Shem, Ham and Japheth.... These were the three sons of Noah, and from them the whole earth was peopled'. Genesis 9, 18–19 According to the Bible, the world was re-populated after the flood by the descendants of Noah's sons. Japheth's peoples lived to the north, Ham's lived in Africa and Canaan, while Shem's children lived in Mesopotamia and were the ancestors of the Israelites. Our word 'semite' is derived from the name 'Shem'.

Some people in the Middle East continue to live as nomadic herders as their ancestors did during biblical times.

The Philistines

The Philistines were one of the Sea Peoples who invaded the Eastern Mediterranean in the 12th century BC (see pp. 22–23).

The head and shoulders portrait (right) is a detail from a brick found at the Temple of Ramesses III in Egypt. The man's distinctive headdress shows that he is a Philistine.

The stele (right) shows an Assyrian official. The Assyrians destroyed the northern kingdom of Israel in 722 BC (see pp. 26–27).

Cush

The kingdom of Cush (modern Ethiopia/Sudan), in Africa, was long dominated by Egypt. Cushites are mentioned several times in the Old Testament. One of Moses's wives was a Cushite woman.

A statue of the Roman Emperor Tiberius.

A gold coin showing an eagle, symbol of Roman power.

The Romans

The Roman general Pompey occupied Jerusalem in 63 BC. From that time onwards Rome had a controlling influence in Palestine, or Judaea, as it was known then (see pp. 38–39, 42–43). The Romans ruled through local leaders, such as Herod, or through Roman governors, such as Pontius Pilate. Although the Romans were tolerant of different religious beliefs, they did require allegiance to the emperor, which the Christians were unable to swear; this led to their persecution.

Bulls were worshipped for their strength and fertility in many early religions. This little statue comes from Elam, in southwestern Iran. It dates from about 2000 BC.

Religions of the Bible Lands

In the biblical tradition, God is very clear about the worship of other gods: *'Thou shalt have no other gods before me. Thou shalt not take unto thee any graven image, or any likeness of anything...'* Exodus 20, 3–4. The Ten Commandments specifically exclude other gods and forbid the worship of idols (statues or symbols of gods). The ancient Hebrews were emphatic about not worshipping other gods because there were so many religious traditions in the Bible Lands besides their own. Although the Hebrew religion shared some of these traditions, it was the first to outlaw all other gods and goddesses. It was 'monotheistic', which means believing that only one God exists. The other traditions all had many gods and goddesses. Some were deities of natural objects or events, such as the moon, the sun or thunder. Others were fertility gods or goddesses related to events like birth and the harvest. Religious customs included erecting an upright stone for worship, or choosing a tree as 'holy' and performing religious ceremonies beneath it. Open-air altars for sacrifice and worship were chosen or constructed, and elaborate temples were built and dedicated to a god or goddess. As societies became more complex, priests and priestesses were appointed to serve the deity and to care for the temple.

This stone with carvings of uplifted hands and a crescent moon comes from a Canaanite temple dedicated to the worship of the moon god and his wife. It dates from about the 13th century BC.

Stela of Baal, from Ugarit. He was usually shown as a young man, often with an arm raised, brandishing a thunderbolt. Alternatively, he was shown as a bull.

Baal

The religious traditions of the ancient Hebrews and the Canaanites have many features in common. Baal was worshipped outdoors in high places and at open-air altars. The Hebrew God was also worshipped in these places, although the practice was strongly discouraged after the construction of the Temple in Jerusalem. The most important Canaanite myth tells how Baal fought against the Chaos monster, Yam, for the kingship of the world. Baal won the battle and gained control over the rains, the seasons and world order. A similar story of God's defeat of a chaos monster appears in the Bible.

The gods of the Philistines

The Philistines were one of the Sea Peoples. They settled in Canaan at about the same time that the Israelites did. Little is known of their religion because they soon assimilated many of the Canaanite divinities. Three Philistine gods are referred to in the Old Testament – Dagon, Ashtoreth (also found in the Ugarit texts) and Beelzebub (clearly related to Baal.)

The gods of Canaan

Little was known about the Canaanite gods until the discovery in 1929 of a hoard of ancient religious texts in Ugarit, in northern Syria. Although Ugarit is not in Canaan, archaeologists believe that the religion was the same further south. The chief god was El, god of the sky and creator of the world. His son, Baal, was a weather god who brought the welcome rains in the autumn. Baal's partner was Astarte (also known as Ashtoreth or Elat). Astarte was a fertility goddess. She was frequently represented by or with sacred trees, or as a cow (like the Egyptian goddess, Hathor).

This very elaborate Canaanite cult stand or altar (right) dates to about the 10th century BC, when the Israelites were already settled in Canaan.

The strangely shaped figure (left) is another representation of the goddess Astarte. Many statues of the fertility goddess have been found in Canaan. This suggests that they were used for daily worship or as household gods.

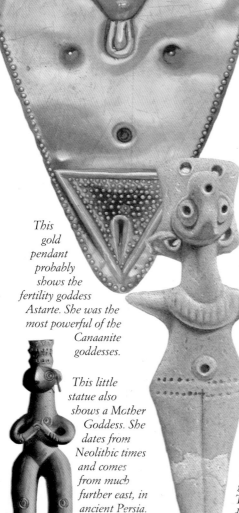

This gold pendant probably shows the fertility goddess Astarte. She was the most powerful of the Canaanite goddesses.

This little statue also shows a Mother Goddess. She dates from Neolithic times and comes from much further east, in ancient Persia.

The Hittite storm god (above) carrying several bolts of lightning and a hammer. The Hittites probably adopted divinities from the local peoples in Anatolia (Turkey) and Syria. The figure shown here is quite similar in function and appearance to the Canaanite god Baal.

A baked earth tablet (above) shows an early Babylonian (2000–1600 BC) war god stabbing a one-eyed sun god. We don't know who the gods are, but it may be a picture of a myth that has since been lost.

Nergal (left), a god from Sumer and Akkad, became king of the underworld. His cult lasted many centuries. He was worshipped as far afield as Canaan and Athens.

The Mesopotamian goddess, Ishtar (left), had very ancient origins.

Mesopotamian king or god with four wings (below).

The ancient Persian god, Zervan, belonged to a religion related to the main Persian religion, Zoroastrianism.

Bas-relief (below) showing a winged demon, perhaps the Babylonian-Assyrian goddess Lilit.

Religion in Mesopotamia

Like most peoples in the ancient world, Mesopotamians believed that the gods controlled everything and that their unpredictable behaviour could be influenced by offerings and prayer. They worshipped divinities of nature, including sun, moon, storm, water and fertility gods and goddesses. Each civilization had its own gods, although many were quite similar and are clearly of common origin.

Egyptian religion

The Egyptians had many gods. Some came from nature, such as Nut, the sky goddess, Geb, the earth god, and Re, the sun god. Others stood for ideas; for example, Thoth was the god of learning and wisdom. The Egyptian king, or pharaoh, was the high priest of all the gods and was a go-between for gods and people. His priests made offerings to the gods so that they would bring good things to Egypt, such as the annual flood and rich crops. The Egyptians believed in life after death and they made elaborate preparations for life in the next world. The bodies of rich people were mummified and buried with many belongings so that the next life would be comfortable.

The Egyptian gods Anubis (left) and Thoth (right) weigh the heart of a dead person to see if he or she has been good during this life.

The Greek goddess of creation, Gaea (left).

Snake goddess (below) from the Minoan civilization that flourished on the island of Crete 2000–1500 BC.

Greek and Roman religion

The Greeks believed their gods lived on Mount Olympus. The supreme god was Zeus (Jupiter), but there were many others. The Romans took over the Greek gods, although they gave them Roman names. The main gods were Apollo, Pluto (Dis), Ares (Mars), Artemis (Diana), Athena (Minerva), Aphrodite (Venus) and Demeter (Ceres).

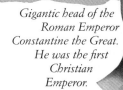

One of the best-known Greek myths tells how Athena (goddess of the powerful city of Athens) was born from the head of the chief god, Zeus. The story is illustrated (above) on a Greek vase.

Gigantic head of the Roman Emperor Constantine the Great. He was the first Christian Emperor.

Household gods, called lares and penates (left), were kept by the Romans. Offerings and prayers were made to them each day.

GREECE

Limits to growth
Egyptian expansion was blocked in the north firstly by the
Mitanni and later by the Hittites. The empire reached its
greatest extent under Pharaoh Tuthmosis II (1504–1450
BC). Two hundred years later the warrior king, Ramesses
II, tried to reconquer northern Syria. He was prevented
from doing so by the Hittites at the Battle of Kadesh.

ANATOLIA

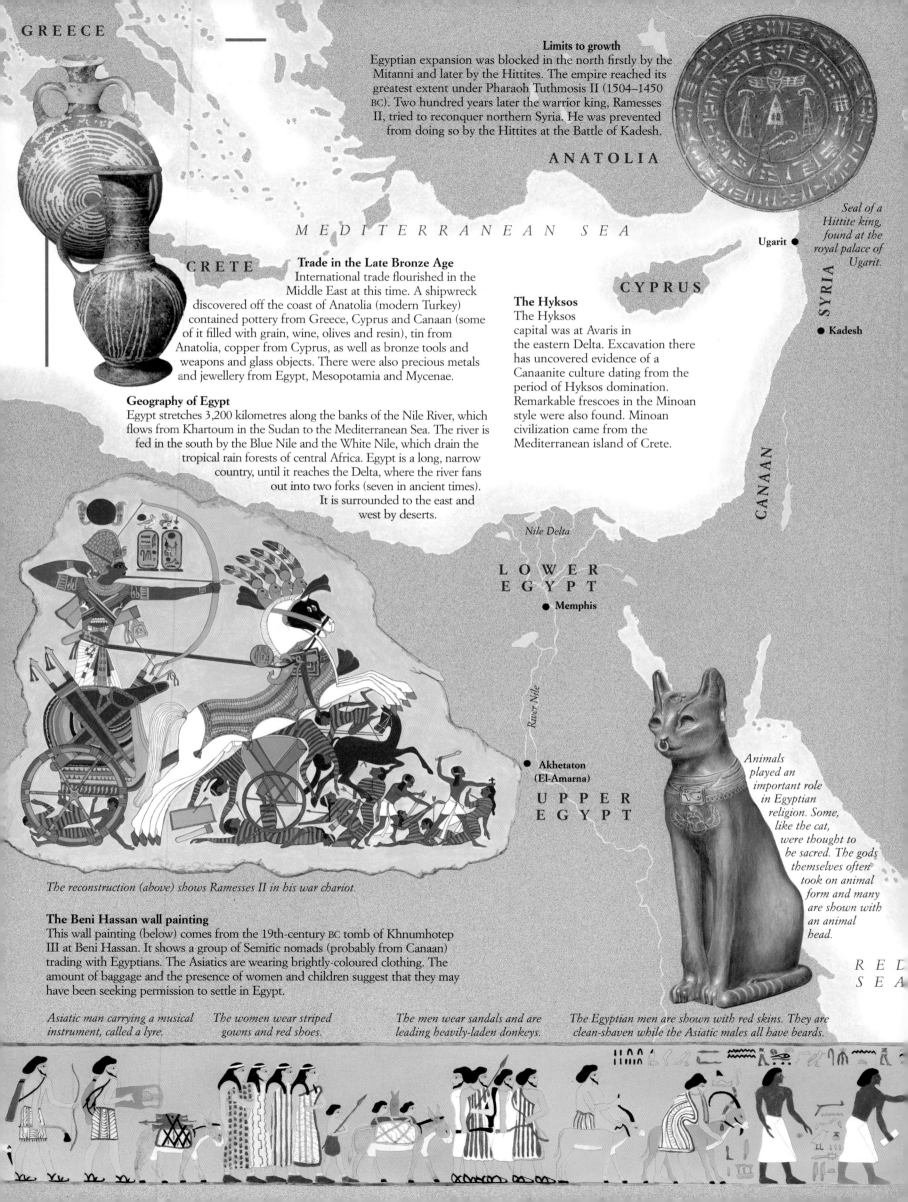

*Seal of a
Hittite king,
found at the
royal palace of
Ugarit.*

MEDITERRANEAN SEA

Ugarit ●

SYRIA

● Kadesh

CRETE

CYPRUS

Trade in the Late Bronze Age
International trade flourished in the
Middle East at this time. A shipwreck
discovered off the coast of Anatolia (modern Turkey)
contained pottery from Greece, Cyprus and Canaan (some
of it filled with grain, wine, olives and resin), tin from
Anatolia, copper from Cyprus, as well as bronze tools and
weapons and glass objects. There were also precious metals
and jewellery from Egypt, Mesopotamia and Mycenae.

The Hyksos
The Hyksos
capital was at Avaris in
the eastern Delta. Excavation there
has uncovered evidence of a
Canaanite culture dating from the
period of Hyksos domination.
Remarkable frescoes in the Minoan
style were also found. Minoan
civilization came from the
Mediterranean island of Crete.

Geography of Egypt
Egypt stretches 3,200 kilometres along the banks of the Nile River, which
flows from Khartoum in the Sudan to the Mediterranean Sea. The river is
fed in the south by the Blue Nile and the White Nile, which drain the
tropical rain forests of central Africa. Egypt is a long, narrow
country, until it reaches the Delta, where the river fans
out into two forks (seven in ancient times).
It is surrounded to the east and
west by deserts.

CANAAN

Nile Delta

LOWER
EGYPT
● Memphis

River Nile

● Akhetaton
(El-Amarna)

UPPER
EGYPT

*Animals
played an
important role
in Egyptian
religion. Some,
like the cat,
were thought to
be sacred. The gods
themselves often
took on animal
form and many
are shown with
an animal
head.*

The reconstruction (above) shows Ramesses II in his war chariot.

RED
SEA

The Beni Hassan wall painting
This wall painting (below) comes from the 19th-century BC tomb of Khnumhotep
III at Beni Hassan. It shows a group of Semitic nomads (probably from Canaan)
trading with Egyptians. The Asiatics are wearing brightly-coloured clothing. The
amount of baggage and the presence of women and children suggest that they may
have been seeking permission to settle in Egypt.

*Asiatic man carrying a musical
instrument, called a lyre.*

*The women wear striped
gowns and red shoes.*

*The men wear sandals and are
leading heavily-laden donkeys.*

*The Egyptian men are shown with red skins. They are
clean-shaven while the Asiatic males all have beards.*

Egypt and Canaan

Ancient Egyptian civilization appeared in the Nile River Valley about 3100 BC. There are records of trade, disputes and diplomatic relations between Egypt and Canaan from earliest times. The Egyptians imported many items, including timber (particularly cedarwood from Lebanon) and other merchandise produced in Canaan or dealt with by its merchants. People from Canaan travelled frequently in Egypt and many of them settled there, especially when there was a drought or famine at home. From the 19th century BC onwards, more and more Canaanites settled in Egypt, particularly in the eastern Delta region. This is when Joseph or other descendants of the patriarchs may have entered Egypt. During the Second Intermediate Period (1750–1550 BC), when Egyptian rule was weak, some of the settlers, whom the Egyptians called Hyksos, took power. They ruled for about 200 years, until they were expelled by Pharaoh Ahmosis, whose reign marked the beginning of the New Kingdom. From then on, Egyptian rulers maintained control over most of Canaan, establishing an empire which lasted for about 400 years.

Stone weights inscribed with their value were used as money. The shekel was the basic unit in Canaan.

The story of Joseph
The Old Testament story tells how Joseph was sold into slavery in Egypt by his brothers for 20 shekels; the exact price for a slave listed on the Hammurabi stela of the 18th century BC. This, and other historical records, have shown that the biblical narration of many events in Joseph's life, including his rise to power in the Egyptian court and his brothers' trading trip to buy corn in Egypt during a famine in Canaan, fit in with the overall picture of life at the time.

Tutankhamun reigned for nine years (1361–52 BC), between the ages of 9–18. His death mask is probably one of the best known pieces of Egyptian art.

Carving of the Pharaoh Akhenaten with his wife Nefertiti. It is a family scene with both parents holding a child. The disc at the top represents the sun god.

Akhenaten – an early monotheist?
The ancient Egyptians worshipped many gods, with the exception of the Pharaoh Amenophis IV (also known as Akhenaten) who ruled from 1379–62 BC. Akhenaten broke with tradition and worshipped just one god, the Aten, or sun god. During his reign he tried to force his views on the rest of Egypt. After his death, the old gods were reinstated.

Egypt's empire
Egyptian rule in Canaan was marked by alternating periods of peace and strife. During peaceful times international trade prospered all over the eastern Mediterranean. Ugarit, a port in Syria, became a major centre of commerce. There was a two-way flow of goods between Egypt and Canaan. Merchants also dealt in items from Greece (Minoan, then Mycenaean), Cyprus, Mesopotamia, Egypt and even further afield. At times the Egyptian grip on Canaan weakened and war broke out among the peoples of Canaan, or against the foreign rulers. A coalition of local peoples was decisively beaten by the Egyptians at the Battle of Megiddo in about 1490 BC. Two hundred years later the Egyptians faced a rival in the Hittite empire to the north of Syria. They fought the Battle of Kadesh in about 1300 BC, and although both sides claimed victory, neither really won.

Fresco showing ancient Egyptians winnowing grain.

The Amarna tablets
The Amarna tablets consist of 380 texts found at El-Amarna in Egypt. Dating from the 14th century BC, they are written in Akkadian (from Mesopotamia, and the international language of the time). They are mainly letters written by or to the Pharaohs Amenophis III, Akhenaten and Tutankhamun (1361–52 BC). The Egyptians had officials posted in many parts of Canaan who wrote to the Egyptian court on a regular basis.

This fresco, dating from the 14th century BC, when Canaan was under Egyptian rule, shows Canaanites offering gifts to the Pharaoh.

Two of the Amarna tablets (left). The tablets are a vital source of information about ancient Egypt and its relationships with neighbouring countries.

Ugarit
The seaport of Ugarit in northern Syria was a major centre of trade and a rich and cosmopolitan city. Much of what we know about Canaan at this time is based on finds from its archives. An early form of alphabet was developed in Ugarit in the 13th century BC.

Egyptian agriculture
As in Mesopotamia, Egyptian civilization depended on agriculture. It relied on the annual flood, which washed fertile silt over the river flats, creating rich farmland. The season of flooding, called *akhet*, was from August to October. It was followed by *peret* from November to February, when the waters receded and crops were grown, and then *shemu* or 'drought' from March to August.

A clay tablet from Ugarit (right).

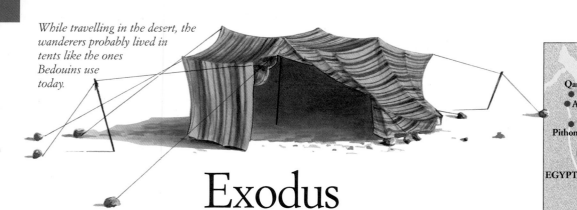

While travelling in the desert, the wanderers probably lived in tents like the ones Bedouins use today.

Exodus

Exodus refers to the Old Testament episode in which Moses leads the Jews out of slavery in Egypt, through the wilderness to the Promised Land of Canaan. Moses died just before they reached Canaan, but during the years of wandering in the desert he founded the religious community known as Israel and was, in the Jewish belief, the interpreter through whom God communicated the laws by which they should live. The story is of great significance in the biblical narrative, but it is surrounded by controversy. Except for the Old Testament, no other evidence has been found to show that the journey took place. Ancient Egyptian records make no mention of a great slave escape, yet according to the Bible 600,000 men and their families fled (an estimated 2 million people!). Because the episode and Moses himself are so important in the Bible, some historians think that many of the events may have taken place, although perhaps over a longer period of time and on a reduced scale.

The clay dish (above) shows the wanderers gathered together to worship with Moses. It was found in the Sinai Desert.

Medieval miniature (left) showing Moses on Mount Sinai presenting the Tables of the Law to the Jews.

Possible routes for the Exodus.
The map shows the four possible routes the Israelites could have taken when fleeing from Egypt on their way to the Promised Land. According to the Bible, they spent many years wandering in the wilderness and lived for a long time at Kadesh Barnea. Archaeologists think this may be the modern oasis of Ein Qudeirat. The location of Mount Sinai, where God appeared to Moses, revealing the Ten Commandments (and, in the Jewish tradition, the text of the Old Testament), is also discussed and many different sites have been proposed.

According to the Bible, the journey through the desert lasted for forty years, much longer than it should have taken. This is because, with a few exceptions, those who left Egypt were not meant to enter the Promised Land.

Locust.

When Aaron threw his staff before the pharaoh it turned into a snake.

The escape
In the Exodus story Moses and Aaron ask the pharaoh to let his Jewish slaves go free. When he refuses, God brings ten plagues down on Egypt, including frogs, boils, hail and locusts. It is only when the tenth plague strikes – the death of all Egyptian firstborn – that the pharaoh agrees to let them leave. As Moses leads his people out of Egypt the Egyptian army follows. The army catches up with them at the Red Sea, but God lets his people cross the sea in safety and drowns the Egyptian army that is chasing them.

The Ark of the Covenant
'Have them make a chest of acacia wood – two and a half cubits long and a half high. Overlay it with pure gold, both inside and out, and make a gold moulding around it. Cast four gold rings for it... Then make poles of acacia wood and overlay them with pure gold. Insert the poles into the rings on the sides of the chest to carry it... Then put in the ark the Testimony, which I will give to you... And make two cherubim out of hammered gold...'. Exodus 25, 10–18.

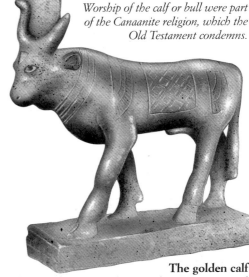

Worship of the calf or bull were part of the Canaanite religion, which the Old Testament condemns.

The golden calf
The people grew impatient when Moses stayed too long on the mountain. They melted down their golden jewellery and made it into the image of a calf with an altar before it. When Moses came down and saw them worshipping the idol he smashed the Tables of the Law and destroyed the calf.

Reconstruction of the Ark based on the very detailed description given in Exodus.

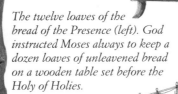

The twelve loaves of the bread of the Presence (left). God instructed Moses always to keep a dozen loaves of unleavened bread on a wooden table set before the Holy of Holies.

THE TABERNACLE

HOLY OF HOLIES

COURTYARD

MENORAH

ARK

The Israelites built a portable worship centre, called the tabernacle, while they were in the Sinai. The inner room, the Holy of Holies, held the Ark. The Israelites worshipped at the tabernacle for centuries, until Solomon built the Temple in Jerusalem.

Horned altar, used for burning incense.

Oil lamp.

Incense shovel.

Turban

Breastplate

Ephod

High priest's clothing (left).

The high priest wore a breastplate (below) inset with twelve jewels engraved with the twelve names of the tribes of Israel.

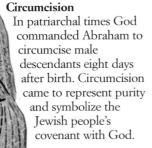

Miniature from the Middle Ages showing a boy about to be circumcised.

Circumcision
In patriarchal times God commanded Abraham to circumcise male descendants eight days after birth. Circumcision came to represent purity and symbolize the Jewish people's covenant with God.

The priesthood
During the Exodus, God appointed the male descendants of Jacob's son Levi to serve in the tabernacle and in the Temple. Later, Aaron and his descendants became priests. The Levites received no land when they arrived in Canaan but lived in the various cities. They were supported for their services by donations and a part of the offerings left in the Temple.

Blue tunic fringed with golden bells.

The Promised Land

A great change came over the eastern Mediterranean during the late 13th to early 12th centuries BC. The Egyptian Empire declined, while the Hittite Empire and many of the city-states of Canaan and Syria, including Ugarit, were destroyed. The island trading centre of Alashiya (Cyprus) was devastated by invaders, while across the Mediterranean, in Greece, the Mycenaean civilization collapsed. It was a period of upheaval and crises, with great movements of populations and refugees. Much of the turmoil was caused by the arrival of huge numbers of migrants, known collectively as the Sea Peoples, from the Aegean and Anatolia. At about the same time, the Israelites (as they had begun to call themselves) were settling in Canaan, the land they believed had been promised to them by God. The Bible refers to the Sea Peoples, but mentions only one group by name – the Philistines. The Philistines were also settling in Canaan at this time and they clashed frequently with the Israelites. Archaeologists think that Canaan was settled gradually by a mixture of Israelite groups, only some of whom arrived from Egypt. The others were probably nomads who had been living there since patriarchal times. The various groups were united as Israelites by their belief in God and their covenant made with him in the desert under Moses's leadership. The Canaanite peoples were either pushed from their land or incorporated into Israel.

The first reference to the nation of Israel outside the Bible appears on an Egyptian stela. Dating to the rule of Pharaoh Merenptah (1231 BC), it describes his campaign in Canaan. Among other victories, he claims to have defeated Israel. The stela says 'Israel is devastated, her seed is no more'.

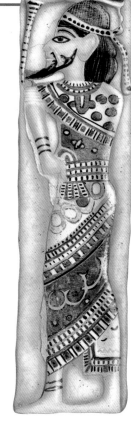

An Egyptian glazed brick shows a Canaanite noble at more or less the time of Israelite settlement.

The destruction of Jericho

'And seven priests shall bear before the ark seven trumpets of rams' horns: and the seventh day ye shall compass the city seven times, and the priests shall blow with the trumpets. And it shall come to pass, that when they make a long blast with the ram's horn, and when ye hear the sound of the trumpet, all the people shall shout with a great shout; and the wall of the city shall fall down flat...' Joshua, 6, 4–5.

The Book of Joshua tells of the miraculous way in which the Israelites captured the city of Jericho. Archaeologists now think that Jericho did not have strong defensive walls in the settlement period, and may even have been uninhabited. However the fact that the 'seige' takes place over seven days, with the Ark and a procession of priests, gives the story a ritual meaning and may refer to the Creation or another important event in the Hebrew tradition.

The end of an era

The decline of the old empires and the beginning of the biblical kingdoms coincides with the introduction of iron into the Middle East. This marks the close of what archaeologists call the Bronze Age and the beginning of the Iron Age (see box on p. 6 for dates). Iron may have been brought in by the Sea Peoples, or it may be that a shortage of copper and tin (the materials used to make bronze) provided the incentive to make iron. In either case, iron was not widely used in the region until the 10th century BC.

This relief statue shows a Philistine warrior with his typical feathered headdress. It comes from the reliefs commissioned by Pharaoh Ramesses III to celebrate his victory over the Sea Peoples. The map shows the population movements in the eastern Mediterranean at this time.

BLACK SEA
AEGEAN SEA
Troy
Mycenae
Boghazköy
Miletus
CRETE
Knossos
Alalakh
Ugarit
SYRIA
Kadesh
MEDITERRANEAN SEA
Dor
CANAAN
LIBYA
Ashdod
EGYPT

The Sea Peoples

Small groups of Sea Peoples had been arriving in the eastern Mediterranean since the 14th century BC. The early groups were absorbed. But in the 12th century BC they came in such large numbers that they conquered the area. As the name suggests, many came by sea, but some must also have journeyed overland, since they are shown in the Ramesses reliefs travelling on ox-carts with women, children and all their possessions aboard. The names of many of the individual tribes are listed in the Ramesses reliefs and another Egyptian papyrus. They include the Philistines, Sherden, Denyen, Weshesh and Tjekker.

The decorations on the Philistine vase (below) are similar to those on pottery produced in the Aegean region. This suggests that the Philistines either came from that area or had frequent trading contacts with the people there.

This unusual cult stand has five musicians peeping from its windows. It shows a mixture of Mycenaean and Canaanite styles, typical of Philistine pottery of the period (early 10th century BC).

A Philistine fertility goddess?

One of the most unusual pieces of Philistine pottery shows a woman whose head and neck are attached to a kind of chair or bed. Although decorated in the Mycenaean style, its shape is unique. Almost nothing is known of early Philistine religion, but scholars think that this piece shows a fertility goddess.

The Philistines

The Philistines settled in southern Canaan. Five major city-states are known: Gaza, Ashkelon, Ashdod, Ekron and Gath. They gradually crept further inland, where they clashed with the Israelites, who were expanding westwards towards the sea. When the Philistines captured the Ark of the Covenant at the Battle of Aphek, the Israelites asked Samuel for a king to unite them against the invaders. Samuel agreed reluctantly, and Saul was made first King of Israel. However, it wasn't until the reign of King David that the Philistines were finally confined to their own territories near the coast. The Philistines disappeared from history in the 6th century BC with the Babylonian invasions, but they have left us a lasting reminder of their presence in one of the common names for the region – 'Palestine' derives from the Latin name for Philistine.

NAPHTALI
ASHER
Dor
Bet She'an
ISSACHAR
MANASSEH
Shiloh
River Jordan
EPHRAIM
GAD
Bethal
Mizpah
Gilgal
BENJAMIN
Jerusalem
Ekron
Ashdod
DAN
REUBEN
Gath
JUDAH
DEAD SEA
Ashkelon
SIMEON
Gaza

This 12th century BC sarcophagus (coffin) in human shape comes from Bet She'an. Many coffins like this one have been found. Some scholars say they were made by the Philistines and other Sea Peoples. This one certainly has Philistine-style headgear. There are also clear signs of Egyptian influence.

The age of the Judges

The settlement of Israel dates to the Early Iron Age, in about 1200–1000 BC. The earliest villages were in the central hill area. Traces of the first shrines of Israel are all in Ephraim (Gilgal, Bethel, Shiloh, Mizpah and Ramah). The first Israelites were subsistence farmers. They cleared the hilltops of native woodland and terraced them for agriculture. They kept livestock and grew wheat, barley, olives and grapes. They lived together in extended family groups composed of husband and wife (or wives), unmarried daughters and their sons and families. The families were associated into larger family groups called clans. The clans were grouped into tribes. In this early period the family or clan was the basic social unit. Government was democratic and decisions were made by general assemblies of men. There were also elders or 'Judges' who acted as leaders to make political and military decisions.

This beautiful ivory carving of a Canaanite girl comes from Megiddo. It dates to the 14th century BC, but the same style and skills continued to be used in Canaan. Similar styles can still be seen in the Phoenician ivories of five centuries later.

This 9th-century BC relief from Syria shows a man with a slingshot. Slingshots were common weapons and could be deadly in war. This is what David would have used to kill the Philistine giant Goliath.

The Age of Kings

Saul was the first King of Israel. He was chosen by Samuel in about 1020 BC. The Israelites appointed a king because they wanted to be united to defend themselves against the Philistines. Little is known of Saul's reign, except that he frequently fought the Philistines and other local kingdoms, and was outwitted regarding his succession by the next King of Israel, David. When Saul died, David became King of Judah in the south, ruling from Hebron. Soon after, Saul's son Ish-Bosheth was assassinated, and the northern tribes also wanted David as their king. The twelve tribes of Israel were united under him. David was a warrior king and he extended the frontiers of Israel in all directions, making it one of the most important kingdoms in the Middle East. He moved the capital to the centrally located city of Jerusalem, after winning the city from the Jebusites. He was succeeded by his son Solomon, another great leader. Solomon inherited a stable kingdom that covered almost all of Canaan. He spent less time than his father at war, devoting his energies to international trade, governing his large empire, building temples and palaces and enlarging his cities.

The conquest of Jerusalem

Jerusalem was only a tiny village when David decided it would make the ideal capital for his newly united kingdom. However, it was protected by sturdy walls. According to legend, David breached the walls and entered the city through the city's water supply systems. Scholars now think this unlikely, since all three systems probably date to the reign of Solomon or later.

The 'House of David' victory stela is the only reference to the dynasty of King David outside the Bible. Three pieces have been found so far. Written in Aramaic, the stela seems to record a victory by Hazael, a king of Aram, over Israel and Judah.

The reign of Solomon

Solomon came to power in about 965 BC. By developing trade and centralizing the administration of his kingdom, he became rich enough to begin a spectacular, nationwide building programme. Besides the work in Jerusalem, he enlarged the cities of Gezer, Hazor and Megiddo. Solomon employed Phoenician craftsmen, but also used a rotating levy of 30,000 men from among the Israelites. This forced labour was hated by many of his subjects.

Solomon's Jerusalem

Solomon enlarged the capital from about 4–5 hectares to about 8–10 hectares. There was no corresponding increase in population. There were probably only about 2,000 inhabitants during Solomon's reign. The new areas were used for monumental buildings. Besides the Temple, he built a cluster of palace buildings, extended the walls and put in at least one of the city's complex water supply systems.

RECONSTRUCTION OF THE CITY OF JERUSALEM AS IT MAY HAVE LOOKED DURING THE REIGN OF SOLOMON.

An Ammonite sculpture, perhaps of a god. He is wearing the atef *crown of Egypt.*

A horned goddess from the Edomite cult centre of Qitmit.

Neighbouring kingdoms

By about 1150 BC **Egypt** no longer ruled over the city-states of Canaan, although it still had influence in the region. In the north, **Aram** was organized in small city-states, including Damascus and Zobah. These city-states controlled the trade routes to and from Egypt, Anatolia and Mesopotamia. Aramaic replaced Akkadian as the main international language. The Aramaeans often fought Israel and Ammon for control of the Transjordan. **Ammon** lay in the Transjordan. It was only a small kingdom but the Ammonites frequently clashed with Israel over control of northern Moab. **Moab** fought often with Ammon, Edom and Israel over territory. But the four kingdoms were sometimes on good terms. In the Bible, the Moabite woman, Ruth, was the ancestor of David. **Edom** lay to the south, controlling access to the Gulf of Eilat. The Bible mentions many other ethnic groups, including the nomadic **Midianites** and **Amalekites**, who influenced Israel.

Jerusalem's water supply came from the Gihon spring in the Kidron valley. Three man-made tunnel systems were built during the First Temple period. They are now known as Warren's Shaft, the Siloam Channel and Hezekiah's Tunnel.

The entrance to Warren's Shaft. The Gihon spring lay outside the city walls and access was gained through a 41-metre tunnel cut through the rock.

Western gate

Solomon's palace and administration buildings

The Temple of Solomon

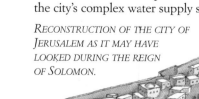

Eastern gate

Stepped stone structure, which acted as a retaining wall, supporting the citadel with the palace and administration centre.

The Phoenicians

Phoenicia lay along the coast of northern Canaan (more or less where Lebanon is today). The Phoenicians were local peoples, of Canaanite origin. Their civilization appeared in about 1200 BC, following the great upheaval at the beginning of the Iron Age. Phoenicia was not a single kingdom but was made up of independent city-states, which is how it is referred to in the Bible.

An early inscription using the Phoenician alphabet.

This relief carving is part of a large work showing the Phoenicians at sea.

The purple people

Our word 'Phoenician' comes from the Greek word *phoinikoi* (people of the purple dye). The colour purple was very rare and expensive to make in the ancient world.

The Phoenicians made it using the murex sea snail, which lived along the coast of Phoenicia. They made two shades of purple – red purple and blue purple – which they traded far and wide.

The Phoenician alphabet

The Phoenicians used an alphabet based on one that developed in southern Canaan during the 17th century BC. Their alphabet gradually spread north into Anatolia and Greece. The Greeks based their alphabet on the Phoenician one, which makes it a direct ancestor of our own alphabet.

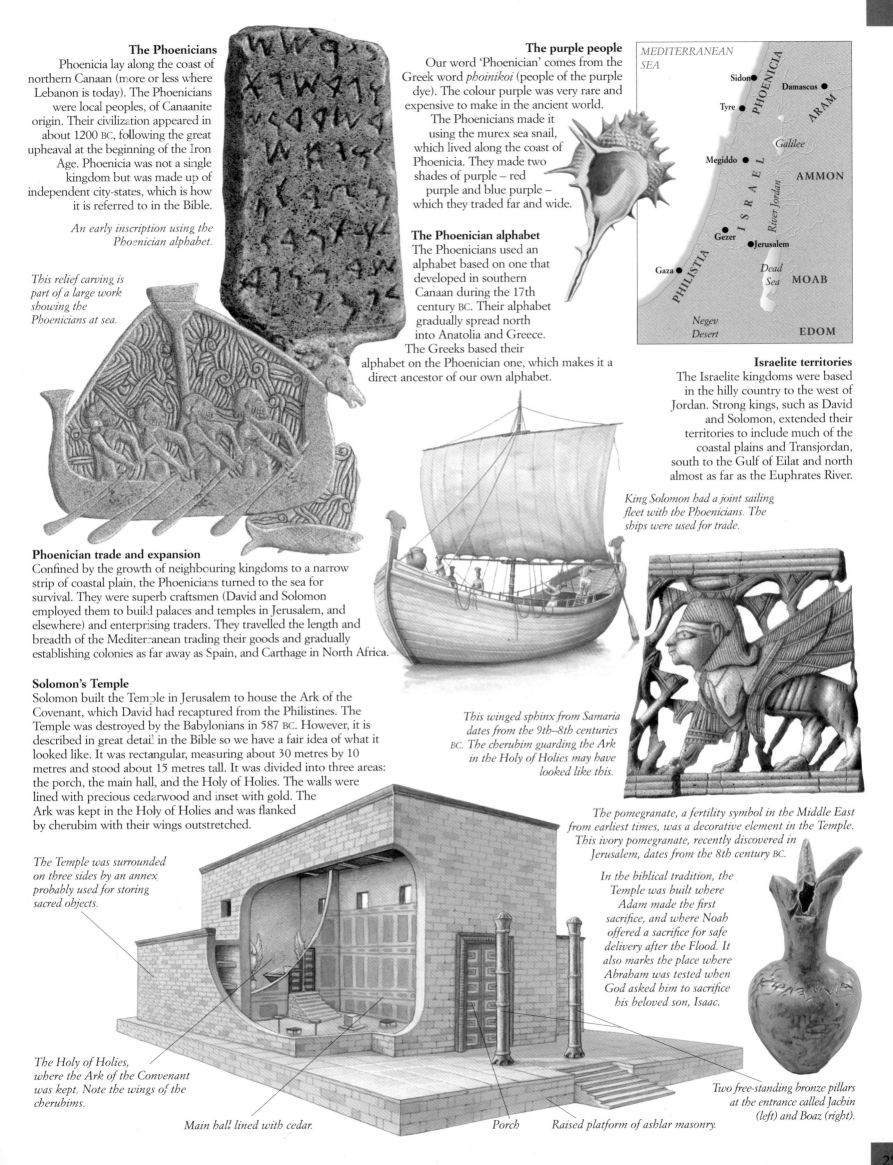

MEDITERRANEAN SEA

Sidon
Damascus
Tyre
PHOENICIA
ARAM
Galilee
Megiddo
AMMON
Gezer
Jerusalem
ISRAEL
River Jordan
Gaza
Dead Sea
MOAB
PHILISTIA
Negev Desert
EDOM

Israelite territories

The Israelite kingdoms were based in the hilly country to the west of Jordan. Strong kings, such as David and Solomon, extended their territories to include much of the coastal plains and Transjordan, south to the Gulf of Eilat and north almost as far as the Euphrates River.

King Solomon had a joint sailing fleet with the Phoenicians. The ships were used for trade.

Phoenician trade and expansion

Confined by the growth of neighbouring kingdoms to a narrow strip of coastal plain, the Phoenicians turned to the sea for survival. They were superb craftsmen (David and Solomon employed them to build palaces and temples in Jerusalem, and elsewhere) and enterprising traders. They travelled the length and breadth of the Mediterranean trading their goods and gradually establishing colonies as far away as Spain, and Carthage in North Africa.

Solomon's Temple

Solomon built the Temple in Jerusalem to house the Ark of the Covenant, which David had recaptured from the Philistines. The Temple was destroyed by the Babylonians in 587 BC. However, it is described in great detail in the Bible so we have a fair idea of what it looked like. It was rectangular, measuring about 30 metres by 10 metres and stood about 15 metres tall. It was divided into three areas: the porch, the main hall, and the Holy of Holies. The walls were lined with precious cedarwood and inset with gold. The Ark was kept in the Holy of Holies and was flanked by cherubim with their wings outstretched.

This winged sphinx from Samaria dates from the 9th–8th centuries BC. The cherubim guarding the Ark in the Holy of Holies may have looked like this.

The pomegranate, a fertility symbol in the Middle East from earliest times, was a decorative element in the Temple. This ivory pomegranate, recently discovered in Jerusalem, dates from the 8th century BC.

The Temple was surrounded on three sides by an annex, probably used for storing sacred objects.

In the biblical tradition, the Temple was built where Adam made the first sacrifice, and where Noah offered a sacrifice for safe delivery after the Flood. It also marks the place where Abraham was tested when God asked him to sacrifice his beloved son, Isaac.

The Holy of Holies, where the Ark of the Convenant was kept. Note the wings of the cherubims.

Main hall lined with cedar.

Porch

Raised platform of ashlar masonry.

Two free-standing bronze pillars at the entrance called Jachin (left) and Boaz (right).

The Divided Kingdom

Golden bracelet belonging to Pharaoh Shishak's son, Prince Nimlot.

When Solomon died in about 928 BC his kingdom split in two. The northern part, thereafter known as the Kingdom of Israel, was much larger and richer than the southern part, known as the Kingdom of Judah. The kingdom split because, under the rebel leader Jeroboam, the north refused to recognize Solomon's son, Rehoboam, unless he promised to reduce taxes and the amount of forced labour on national building projects. When Rehoboam refused, the north seceded. The two kingdoms were never reunited, although they sometimes joined forces against a common enemy. The Kingdom of Israel existed for another two hundred years, until it was conquered by the Assyrians in 722 BC. The Kingdom of Judah continued under the Davidic dynasty for about 350 years, until it came under Babylonian control.

Sargon II of Assyria ruled from 721–705 BC. By the time he took power, the Kingdom of Israel was almost completely under Assyrian control. This relief comes from his palace at Khorsabad. The original carving is almost 1 metre tall. Judging by the attention to detail in the face, it is probably a portrait rather than an idealized representation.

The Moabite Stone (left) records the victory of King Mesha of Moab over a coalition of Israelite, Judean and Edomite troops who sought to put down a Moabite rebellion just after Ahab's death. The inscription is written in Moabite, a language closely related to ancient Hebrew.

Exploiting the weakness of the Divided Kingdom

Judah and Israel fought almost continually during the first decades after the division. This made them both weak and their neighbours, including Egypt, Moab, Ammon and others, were not slow to take advantage of this. Pharaoh Shishak I of Egypt invaded in 924 BC, capturing many cities, including Jerusalem. '*And it came to pass that Shishak king of Egypt came up against Jerusalem and he took away the treasures of the house of the Lord, and the treasures of the king's house; he even took away all...*' I. Kings 25–26. Once he had plundered the main cities and gained control of lucrative trade routes, he returned to Egypt.

Israel worships other gods

Jeroboam, the first King of Israel, built two large shrines, at Dan and Bethel, in the north and south (respectively) of the new Kingdom. These were meant to replace Jerusalem in the minds of his people. Both shrines contained golden calves, which may mean that the inhabitants also worshipped the traditional gods of Canaan.

The House of Omri

The military leader Omri took control of Israel in 882 BC after a civil war. He and his son Ahab introduced a period of relative stability. Ahab's sons were murdered by Joram, a military commander. Joram came to power in 842 BC but was almost immediately forced to pay tribute to the Assyrians.

Peace before the storm

The Assyrian threat retreated in the early 8th century BC when the Easterners' attention was fixed on the situation in Anatolia. It was a time of peace and prosperity for both Judah and Israel. They regained control of trade routes and territories that almost equalled those of the times of David and Solomon.

This bronze bull was found at Samaria. Figures of bulls and calves are traditionally associated with the worship of the Canaanite god Baal, of whom the bull was a common symbol. The calves erected in the shrines at Dan and Bethel may have been like this one.

Megiddo

Megiddo, strategically positioned on one of the main routes to the sea, was an important religious and commercial centre from about 3000 BC onwards. It was enlarged under David and Solomon and again under the House of Omri.

New capital in Samaria

King Omri moved the capital of the Kingdom of Israel to Samaria. He and Ahab extended the city considerably. Ahab employed many Phoenician craftsmen and the city had a strong northern flavour. Ahab also undertook substantial building programmes in Hazor and Megiddo. Both cities were important for defence and administration, as they had been under Solomon. Archaeologists have uncovered large storehouses, as well as collections of carved ivory objects similar to the ones found in Samaria.

Reconstruction of the storehouses of Megiddo, probably used to keep produce collected as taxation.

Storeroom where over 200 fragments of ivories were found, plus 65 pottery fragments inscribed in ancient Hebrew, listing the capacity and owners of the wine-jars, probably for taxation.

The royal palace. It consisted of a central courtyard with a large pool, and many rooms.

Square platform, probably the foundation of a tower.

MAP OF THE WESTERN PART OF THE CITY OF SAMARIA AS IT MUST HAVE LOOKED AT THE TIME OF OMRI AND AHAB.

Round tower; may date from later.

Ahab married a Phoenician woman, Jezebel. His daughter, Athaliah, married Jeroham, King of Judah, establishing an alliance between the divided kingdoms. Both women encouraged the worship of Baal. Athaliah even introduced a sanctuary of Baal into the Temple in Jerusalem. The traditional 'woman at a window' motif in Phoenician and Assyrian art (above) has become associated with the name of Jezebel. Jezebel remained loyal to her Canaanite gods until her death and was reviled in the Bible because of this.

The Assyrians

The fertile plains of the Tigris River, near the city of Nineveh, were the heartland of the mighty Assyrian Empire. Dating back to the 3rd millenium BC, Assyria began its new drive for empire in the 9th century BC. Expanding both east and west, by 669 BC its frontiers included the entire Fertile Crescent, from the Persian Gulf to the Nile Valley.

Hunting was a favourite pastime of Assyrian kings and noblemen. Lions were plentiful in the Middle East at the time and were the preferred prey.

The fall of Samaria

After two centuries of independence, the Kingdom of Israel ceased to exist in 722 BC. The capital, Samaria, was captured and its inhabitants sent into exile in various parts of the Assyrian Empire. The Assyrian leader Sargon II wrote: '*In the beginning of my royal rule, I besieged and conquered the city of the Samarians.... I led away 27,290 of its inhabitants as captives... I have rebuilt the city better than it had been before and settled it with people which I brought from the lands of my conquests. I have put an officer of mine as their lord, and imposed upon them a tribute as on other Assyrian subjects*'.

The Assyrian army

The Assyrian army was organized according to a strict hierarchy and its men were well-equipped with armour, shields, bows and arrows, slingshots, spears, swords and chariots as befitting their position and rank.

Reconstruction of the bronze armour that the Assyrians wore in battle.

Statue of the Assyrian god Lahmu. Tiny statues like this one were often used in the home as protection against evil spirits.

MEDITERRANEAN SEA

CYPRUS

Carchemish

SYRIA

Damascus

ASSYRIA

Nineveh

Nimrud

Assur

Euphrates

Tigris

Babylon

BABYLONIA

Jerusalem

Lachish

Nile

EGYPT

This leaping figure of a lion comes from the reliefs at Nineveh. The lion (lord of the desert) was a common symbol in Assyria, along with the eagle (queen of the sky) and the bull (a fertility symbol). Statues or images of these animals are common. They are often of colossal size.

Relief statue (right) of the Sumerian hero Gilgamesh, as he tames a lion cub. From the palace at Khorsabad, it dates from the 8th century BC.

PERSIAN GULF

Judah alone

When the northern Kingdom of Israel fell, many refugees fled south to Judah. The population increased greatly at this time. King Hezekiah came to power in Judah not long before the fall of Samaria. He set about enlarging his cities to absorb the new arrivals, and fortifying them against Assyrian attack. Jerusalem was significantly enlarged and its water supply system reorganized. King Hezekiah formed an anti-Assyrian league with Egypt and some smaller kingdoms and revolted against the Assyrians in 701 BC. The Assyrian leader, Sennecherib, (Sargon's son) reacted immediately, marching down the coast towards Judah. He defeated city after walled city (46 according to the Assyrians), but although Jerusalem was attacked, it survived.

The siege of Lachish

The city of Lachish, to the south of Jerusalem, was not as lucky as the capital. The Assyrians laid siege to the city, breaching the walls with their fearsome battering rams and then looting and terrorizing the people within. The siege is clearly documented in the reliefs from Nineveh (now in the British Museum). The scene below shows some of the luckier inhabitants, who escaped with their families and worldly goods, filing glumly out the city gates.

Head
of a ceremonial axe
made of bronze. Skilled
craftspeople and blacksmiths used
gold, silver, copper, bronze and iron to
make tools and ornaments.

Large and small clay jugs
like this one, dating from the
12th century BC, were used
to store and serve oil, wine
or water. Wine, made of
grapes but also of other
fruit such as dates, was drunk for pleasure
and also used as a medicine. The grape
harvest was a joyous occasion that took
place in August and September. Grapes
were trodden by foot or crushed in presses.

Cloth head
covering

Tunic

Simple
belt

Leather
sandals

Clothing
Clothing was made from linen,
sheep's wool, goats' hair and
animal skins. The materials were
woven and spun into fabric.
Spinning and weaving were done
by women. They used a hand
spindle to spin the wool or linen
into thread and then a loom to
weave it into cloth. Wool was
often dyed to make brightly-
coloured cloth. If the weaver was
working on a large loom, the
garments were woven in one
piece. On a smaller loom they
were woven in three pieces, which
were sewn together.

Crafts and Technology

The first Israelite settlers in Canaan were self-sufficient.
Their small hilltop farms produced just enough food to
feed their families. Domestic animals such as sheep, goats
and cattle produced meat and milk, and also wool and
leather for clothing and footwear. Craftspeople, or the
farmers themselves, produced metal tools for agriculture,
metal and pottery utensils, and storage jars for food
production. Canaan was a dry land, particularly in the
hilly part where the first Israelites settled. They relied on
rainfall and springs. Lack of water meant that only small-
scale irrigation schemes were in use. By the time of kings
David and Solomon things had changed. Israel was much
larger and it owned more fertile terrain near the
coasts. It also took part in international trade,
importing linen and cloths, metals, spices and gold
from abroad.

Hair, headdress and footwear
Israelites wore their hair long in
Old Testament times. Because
the sun was so hot they usually
wore a piece of cloth on their
heads, folded so that it protected
the neck, head and eyes. It was
held in place by a piece of
plaited wool. Sandals were the
most common type of footwear,
although poor people probably
went barefoot.

Cloth
headgear
with plaited
strip of wool to
hold the cloth
in place.

Cloth
folded into a
belt where
personal
belongings
could be
kept.

Purse

Stick

Middle Eastern traders
used the one-humped
Arabian camel for their
caravans. But traders
from far-off central
Asia with the two-
humped camels were
not an uncommon sight.

Trade
When the Israelites first settled in Canaan they were poor farmers, producing
only enough food to feed their families. By the time of King Solomon they
were exporting oil, cereals, wool, clothing, nuts and honey to neighbouring
countries. They imported basics, such as timber, linen and tin, but also
luxury items, including ivory, spices, and exotic animals. Israel stood at the
crossroads of many international trade routes. Nomadic desert tribesmen
carried goods to and from Israel by camel caravan. Goods were also sent by
sea to various parts of the Mediterranean.

Leather
sandals

Clothing styles
Both men and women wore long,
simple tunics reaching to their
calves or ankles. The tunic was
fastened at the waist with a piece
of cloth, folded into a long strip
to form a kind of pocket to
hold coins and personal
belongings. A rich man
might have had a leather
belt with a dagger.

Spices were luxury goods imported from
the East. Cinnamon, for example,
came all the way from India by
an overland route.

Bronze
lion-weight
from Nimrud
in Assyria.

Clay model of
a woman
forming dough
into loaves from
ez-Zib in
northern
Israel. It dates
to the 8th
century BC.

Lighting was provided by lamps in
which fish or vegetable oils
were burned. The lamp
(above) dates from
patriarchal
times.

Water

Water is a scarce resource in Palestine. The ancient Hebrews depended mainly on rain to supply them with water for drinking, household use and farming. The lack of large rivers meant that irrigation schemes were small and usually fed by hillside springs. In other parts of the Middle East, such as Egypt and Mesopotamia, where there were large rivers flowing through the deserts, wide use was made of irrigation for farming.

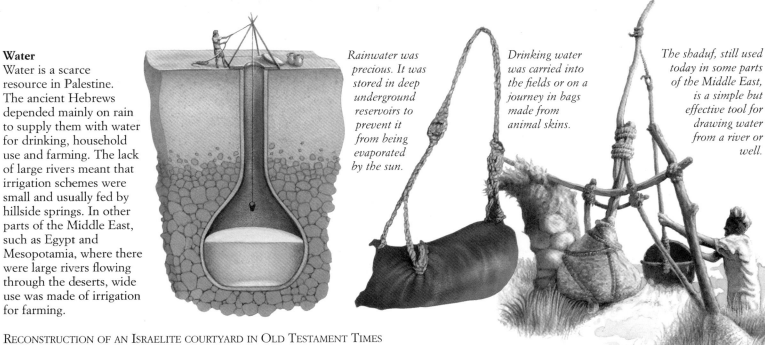

Rainwater was precious. It was stored in deep underground reservoirs to prevent it from being evaporated by the sun.

Drinking water was carried into the fields or on a journey in bags made from animal skins.

The shaduf, still used today in some parts of the Middle East, is a simple but effective tool for drawing water from a river or well.

RECONSTRUCTION OF AN ISRAELITE COURTYARD IN OLD TESTAMENT TIMES

Press for crushing olives to make oil. A sturdy beam was fixed to the outer wall. It was weighted at the end so that it pressed down on wicker baskets full of olives and covered with a heavy stone. The oil was caught in a hollow at the base and funnelled into a well cut into the courtyard floor.

A large oven like this one would have been used to bake bread for the whole village.

Oil jar with a dipper.

Weights for the press.

Basket of olives waiting to be pressed.

Kneading dough to make bread.

Cooking pots

Water jug

Hollow in the floor to collect the oil or juice.

Pestle and mortar, for crushing grain.

Quern, for crushing grain.

Weight, measures and money

Until coins were invented in the 7th century BC, people exchanged goods of equal value without using money. Gold and silver were stored as jewellery rather than as coins, and flocks of sheep or goats were common items of exchange. But these things were cumbersome to exchange. Gradually, a system of metal weights, made of gold, silver, copper and bronze, began to be used for exchange. The metals were formed into lumps or shapes that could be carried in bags. Buyers and sellers each carried weights so that they could check that they were not being cheated.

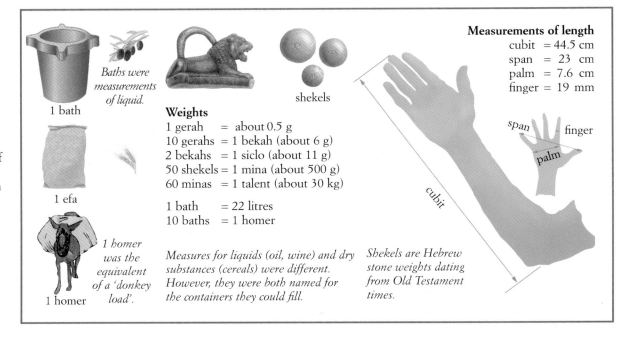

Baths were measurements of liquid.

1 bath

1 efa

1 homer was the equivalent of a 'donkey load'.

1 homer

shekels

Weights

1 gerah	=	about 0.5 g
10 gerahs	=	1 bekah (about 6 g)
2 bekahs	=	1 siclo (about 11 g)
50 shekels	=	1 mina (about 500 g)
60 minas	=	1 talent (about 30 kg)
1 bath	=	22 litres
10 baths	=	1 homer

Measures for liquids (oil, wine) and dry substances (cereals) were different. However, they were both named for the containers they could fill.

Shekels are Hebrew stone weights dating from Old Testament times.

Measurements of length

cubit	=	44.5 cm
span	=	23 cm
palm	=	7.6 cm
finger	=	19 mm

span finger

palm

cubit

Daily Life in Old Testament Times

Mosaic floor showing common religious objects: a menorah (seven-branched candle holder), a palm branch, an incense shovel and the shofar. From the synagogue at Hammath-Tiberias.

The shofar, a wind instrument made from ram's horn, was blown to sound an alarm, give signals in war, announce a king's coronation and to proclaim the year of jubilee and the new and full moons. It is still used in synagogues today.

Most people lived in villages or small towns and worked as farmers in Old Testament times. They owned land outside the settlement and the rhythms of daily life were set by the seasons and the work in the fields. There was always plenty to do. Some of the main jobs were ploughing, sowing seeds, weeding, harrowing, pruning, picking fruit, harvesting grain and flax, crushing olives to make oil and preserving and storing the produce. Most families kept at least some sheep and goats that grazed in the surrounding countryside. Children helped to watch over them. But life was not all work. The ancient calendar was punctuated with sacred feast days and festivals. There were commemorations of important events in the history of the Jewish people, such as the Exodus. There were also celebrations of agricultural activities, such as the harvest, and of family events, including birth and marriage. The Sabbath, a day of rest on the seventh day of each week, was a special time for the family, servants and even the animals. The festivals from this time are still celebrated by Jews today.

Land ownership

When the Israelites settled in Canaan, they distributed the land evenly. One plot was given to each family and was handed down from father to son. If a family fell on hard times it was the duty of a close relative to buy the land to keep it in the family. Under David and Solomon a wealthy landowning class developed and bought up large areas of land. Poor people without land were oppressed and had to work on the large estates to survive.

Feasts and fasting

The main festivals are shown below. The first day of each month was also a feast day. Trumpets were blown and sacrifices made. There were special meals and religious teaching. The Day of Atonement was a day of fasting. Six other fast days were set aside in remembrance of tragic events. People also fasted in times of difficulty or as a sign of repentance.

Pentecost or Weeks

Celebrated 50 days after Passover. In biblical times it marked the season of the wheat harvest and was known as the 'Harvest feast' or the 'Day of the First Fruits'. It also came to mark the day that Moses received God's laws on Mount Sinai.

Passover

Celebrated on the eve of the 14th day of Nisan (March/April), Passover was (and still is) one of the most important festivals. In biblical times a lamb was sacrificed as a reminder of the time God 'passed over' Jewish families in Egypt, sparing their first-born sons. Unleavened bread was eaten with the Passover meal and throughout the following week in memory of the Exodus. It was also a spring festival. On the second day of Passover an offering of barley was made in the Temple.

Trumpets (later, New Year) *The first day of the seventh month (Tishri, counting from Nisan) was a special day of rest and worship. Trumpets were blown extra long and hard on the first day of this month. After the return from Exile, it became a New Year festival.*

Day of Atonement *The people of Israel asked God's forgiveness for their sins. The high priest sent a goat off into the desert (the 'scapegoat'), as a sign that the people's sins had been taken away.*

Children

Children were highly valued and women who did not have them were often scorned. Boys were preferred to girls because they continued the family line. Education was important for Jewish children from earliest times. At first they were taught at home by their parents. Later there were special schools run by the local rabbis. A very high percentage of ancient Hebrews were able to read and write.

The Festival of Tabernacles or Booths *This festival celebrates the wanderings in the wilderness after the Hebrews left Egypt. Special outdoor booths built of tree branches were the scene of joyful celebrations. The feast also marked the end of the agricultural year and was known as the 'Feast of the Ingathering'.*

Festival of Dedication or Lights *This festival dates from after 165 BC, and commemorates the re-dedication of the Second Temple after it had been defiled by Antiochus IV Epiphanes. Eight candles are lit to celebrate.*

The Gezer Calendar *(centre of the diagram) is a list of the agricultural activities for each season of the year. Dating from the 10th century BC, it is scratched into a soft limestone tablet.*

Purim or Festival of Lots *Celebrates the victory of the Hebrew Queen Esther, wife of the Persian King Ahasuerus, who thwarted an attempt by one of the king's officials to massacre the Jews in Persia. The story is told in the Bible in the Book of Esther.*

TRUMPETS (NEW YEAR)

ELUL · TISHRI · HESHVAN · KISLEV · TEVET · SHEVAT · ADAR · NISAN · IYYAR · SIVAN · TAMMUZ · AV

AUGUST · SEPTEMBER · OCTOBER · NOVEMBER · DECEMBER · JANUARY · FEBRUARY · MARCH · APRIL · MAY · JUNE · JULY

A Purim scroll

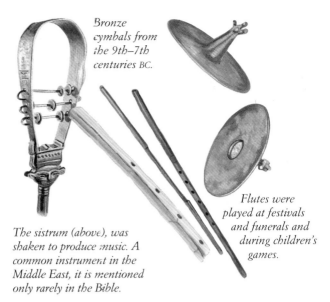

Bronze cymbals from the 9th–7th centuries BC.

The sistrum (above), was shaken to produce music. A common instrument in the Middle East, it is mentioned only rarely in the Bible.

Flutes were played at festivals and funerals and during children's games.

An Israelite home

A typical Israelite home in Old Testament times was a four-roomed structure built of mud brick and arranged around an uncovered central courtyard. Most household tasks were carried out in the courtyard or on the flat roofs above it. Wooden or stone staircases led up to the roofs. The rooms were mainly used for storage or for shelter in bad weather. Cooking, eating and even sleeping were outdoor activities throughout most of the year.

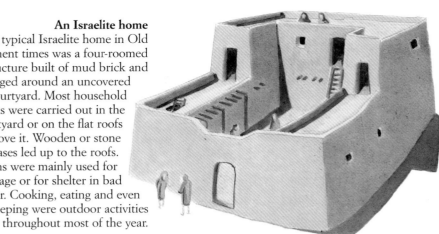

Bread was a staple food throughout the Bible Lands. Making bread was a long job. First the wheat (or barley, if the family was poor) was ground into flour. This was mixed with water and salt, then with yeast from the previous day's baking to make it rise. After the dough had been kneaded, it was shaped into loaves and left to rise. The loaves were baked in an outdoor oven in the courtyard.

Marriage

People married young in Old Testament times. Marriages were arranged by parents, who preferred to find a partner within the same clan so that family wealth was not dispersed. Marriage to someone of another religious group was discouraged. When the families had agreed on a union, a betrothal (engagement) contract was made in front of two witnesses. This agreement was as binding as the wedding ceremony itself. The groom's father paid a bride price to the bride's family to make up for losing her. Sometimes the groom would work for the bride's family to pay this off. The bride's family gave a dowry to the groom, although he was not allowed to spend this; it was returned to the bride if her husband died or if she was divorced. Men were allowed to have more than one wife and wealthy men often had several.

Dietary laws

'Whatsoever parteth the hoof, and is clovenfooted, and cheweth the cud, among the beasts, that shall ye eat'. Leviticus 11, 3.
The books of the Old Testament set down the laws of what should be eaten and what should not be eaten very clearly. They are still observed by orthodox Jews today. Briefly, according to these laws, all plants can be eaten, all meat must be bled, and all animals are either 'clean' or 'unclean'. Unclean mammals include those that feed on the flesh of other creatures, and those that live in more than one of the natural elements (earth, sea, air). Clean mammals have cloven (split) hooves and chew their cuds. Among birds, predators and nocturnal birds cannot be eaten. Fish with fins and scales can be eaten, but other seafoods, such as shellfish, are considered unclean. Another law prohibits eating meat and dairy products at the same meal. There are other laws, as well as many subtle interpretations of those listed above. Finally, the Jews were forbidden to dine with non-Jews.

Women's lives

Women were responsible for running the household. They fetched water from wells, ground grain into flour, cooked meals, made simple household pots and equipment, spun and wove clothing for the family and cared for children and animals. They sometimes worked in the fields and tended flocks. A wife (or wives), concubines and slaves all lived together in the same house; wives had higher status than the other women but they all did the same chores. If a wife was unable to have children, she might raise one or more of the other women's children as her own.

Wedding celebrations could last for up to a week, depending on the wealth of the families. Guests banqueted on fine food and wine and there was often music and dancing too.

Babylonia and Exile

The first king of the new Babylonian Empire was Nabopolassar. He conquered the city of Babylon, freeing it from Assyrian control in 626 BC. He went on to conquer the rest of the Assyrian Empire. Judah became a subject state in 605 BC. Jerusalem was surrendered to the second Babylonian king, Nebuchadrezzar, in 597 BC. The city's leading citizens were exiled to Babylon. Ten years later Jerusalem rebelled. The Babylonians invaded and, after an 18-month-long siege, they finally took Jerusalem. The city, including the Temple, was destroyed. Nearly all the citizens were deported to Babylonia. Valuable objects from the Temple were also sent to Babylon. This period is known in the biblical tradition as 'the exile'.

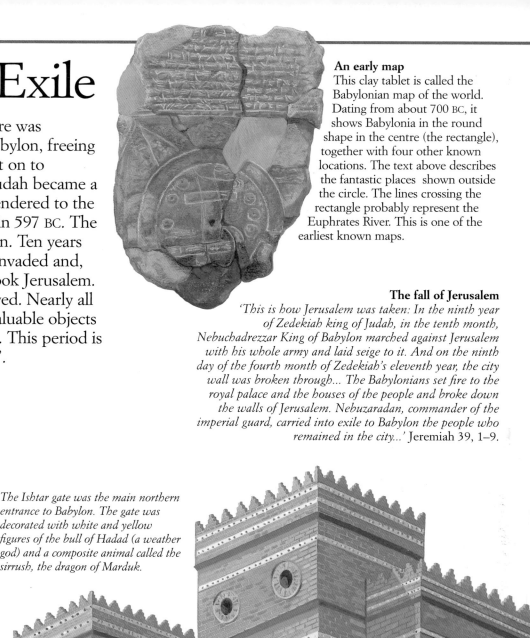

An early map
This clay tablet is called the Babylonian map of the world. Dating from about 700 BC, it shows Babylonia in the round shape in the centre (the rectangle), together with four other known locations. The text above describes the fantastic places shown outside the circle. The lines crossing the rectangle probably represent the Euphrates River. This is one of the earliest known maps.

The fall of Jerusalem
'This is how Jerusalem was taken: In the ninth year of Zedekiah king of Judah, in the tenth month, Nebuchadrezzar King of Babylon marched against Jerusalem with his whole army and laid seige to it. And on the ninth day of the fourth month of Zedekiah's eleventh year, the city wall was broken through... The Babylonians set fire to the royal palace and the houses of the people and broke down the walls of Jerusalem. Nebuzaradan, commander of the imperial guard, carried into exile to Babylon the people who remained in the city...' Jeremiah 39, 1–9.

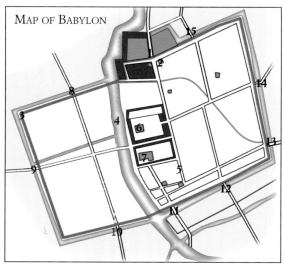

MAP OF BABYLON

1. Ishtar gate
2. Emah temple
3. Ramparts
4. Euphrates river
5. Processional way
6. Tower of Babel
7. Marduk's temple
8. Lugalgirra gate
9. Adad gate
10. Shmash gate
11. Urash gate
12. Enlil gate
13. Zababa gate
14. Marduk gate
15. Sin gate

The city of Babylon
When the Jewish exiles arrived in Babylon it was already an ancient city. It was probably built (or rebuilt) in the 18th century BC by Hammurabi, as the capital of the newly united kingdom of Sumer and Akkad. It stood on the Euphrates River, which was an important transport route for the city. Both Nabopolassar and Nebuchadrezzar spent a great deal of money rebuilding the capital of their empire. The Greek historian, Herodotus, visited Babylon in the 5th century BC. He describes it as a place of incredible splendour, sophistication and wealth. The fame of many of its buildings – the Hanging Gardens, the Ishtar gate, the Tower of Babel and the Royal Palace – is so great that they are still known today. The Tower of Babel, dedicated to the city's god, Marduk, stood on top of a tall ziggurat.

The Ishtar gate was the main northern entrance to Babylon. The gate was decorated with white and yellow figures of the bull of Hadad (a weather god) and a composite animal called the sirrush, the dragon of Marduk.

The 9th-century BC wall carving (right) comes from the royal palace at Nimrud. It shows the king's servants in four different scenes as they prepare the royal meal.

The carved stone (above) was found in Babylon. It shows the sun god Shamash sitting on a throne as he receives King Nabu-apla-iddina and two other gods. The symbol at the centre represents the sun.

This boundary stone comes from Old Babylonian times. It records an agreement about land ownership. It is beautifully decorated with symbols of Babylonian gods and goddesses.

Jewish life in exile
Although the exiles were forbidden to return home, they were not badly treated in other respects. They lived together in their own areas of Babylon and other towns. They were free to build their own houses and to work at the jobs they chose. They were also free to observe their own religion. Some Jews, like Daniel in the Bible, rose to high positions in the Babylonian Government.

The prophets
Some of the captives were content in their new lives and forgot about Judah and Jerusalem. Others never forgot. They were devastated by the loss of the temple and wondered if their God had abandoned them forever because of their wickedness and disobedience. In the Bible, the prophet Ezekiel was with the exiles in Babylon and he promised them that their punishment would end and they would return to their homeland.

The captivity
'By the rivers of Babylon we sat and wept when we remembered Zion. (...) If I forget you, O Jerusalem, may my right hand forget its skill... if I do not remember you, if I do not consider Jerusalem my highest joy'. Psalm 137, 1–6.

• Nineveh

• Babylon

Euphrates River

Tigris River

Damascus •

Jerusalem •

THE PERSIAN GULF

THE RED SEA

Reconstruction of the Hanging Gardens of Babylon.

The Hanging Gardens of Babylon
The Hanging Gardens of Babylon were famous throughout the ancient world. A list drawn up in the second century BC included them as one of the Seven Wonders of the World. The gardens were built within the walls of the royal palace. They did not actually 'hang', but were terraced roof gardens that were irrigated with water pumped from the nearby Euphrates River. According to legend, King Nebuchadrezzar II built the gardens to console his wife, Amytis, who missed the greenery of her mountain home in Media.

The Bible

Our word 'Bible' derives from Greek and Latin words which mean 'books' (*biblia*). This is a good way of describing the Bible, because it is a collection of books written between about 1000 BC and AD 100. The Bible is divided in two parts: the Old Testament and the New Testament. The former, written mainly in Hebrew, is sacred for both Jews and Christians. The latter, written in Greek, is the spiritual foundation of Christianity. It is composed of writings on the life and teachings of Christ (the Gospels) and other writings by Jesus's followers. The Bible is also sacred for Muslims. Over the centuries, the Bible has been translated many times into almost all the written languages of the world. Among the most famous translations are the Greek Septuagint, translated by seventy scholars in the ancient Egyptian library at Alexandria, the Latin Vulgate, translated by Saint Jerome in about AD 400, and the 16th-century German translation by Martin Luther, founder of the Protestant Church.

A Qumran scroll with writings from the Bible and diagrams showing how the scrolls were rolled and tied.

Terracotta jars (right) in which the parchment Qumran scrolls were stored. It was a good way to preserve them; many have survived almost 2,000 years.

The Dead Sea Scrolls

In 1947 archaeologists working at Qumran, on the shores of the Dead Sea, found a site that was occupied between the 2nd century BC and AD 68 by a community of Essenes. The Essenes were a religious sect or brotherhood. They believed that the Temple of Jerusalem had been made unclean by the ruling Hasmonaean dynasty. The Essenes moved away to an abandoned fort at Qumran, which had been turned into a monastery. There they led a simple yet strict life of prayer and meditation. The monastery had a well-stocked library. In AD 68 the library was hidden in nearby caves so that it would not be destroyed by Roman legions, who were putting down the First Jewish revolt. About 800 manuscripts have been found so far. Written on parchment, papyrus and copper, the scrolls contain the entire Bible, as well as many Essene texts.

THE BIBLE

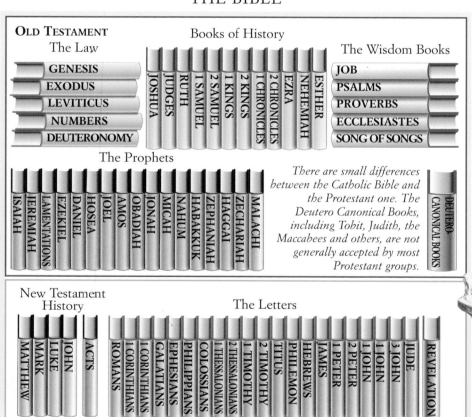

The diagram (above) shows the way the Books of the Bible are arranged in the Christian Bible.

There are small differences between the Catholic Bible and the Protestant one. The Deutero Canonical Books, including Tobit, Judith, the Maccabees and others, are not generally accepted by most Protestant groups.

The making of the Bible

For believers, the Bible is a work inspired by God. Although we don't really know who wrote the various books, in the biblical tradition they are all attributed to certain people. The first five books in the Old Testament, known as the Torah or Pentateuch, are said to be the work of Moses. They tell the story of mankind from the Creation until Moses's death just before the Hebrews occupied Canaan. The next part of the Bible tells how the Hebrews conquered Canaan and lived there until Jerusalem was captured by the Babylonians. Some of these books and many of the ones that follow this historical section are said to have been written by the Prophets and most of them are named after the prophet whose story is told. The Books of the Old Testament cover a period of about 1,000 years. The New Testament was probably written in the span of about 100 years. It is much shorter than the Old Testament. It begins with the four gospels of Matthew, Mark, Luke and John. The other books, with the exception of Acts and The Revelation, are called The Letters.

The ink pot (above), found at Qumran, shows that it is likely that many of the manuscripts were written by scribes of the Qumran community.

Miniature from the Lindisfarne codex, made in Ireland in the 7th century. It shows Saint Mark writing his Gospel.

Writing the Bible

The Bible was written over a period of about 1,100 years. Although most of the authors are unknown, many books are attributed to people of the time. The earliest writers recorded the traditions of the Jewish people, which were previously handed down from parents to their children by word of mouth. The books are not in the order in which they were written.

The bowl (below) is inscribed with magic formulas and biblical verses in Aramaic, one of the languages in which the Bible was written.

A scroll with texts from the Jewish Torah.

The Flood

This clay tablet (right), found at Nineveh in ancient Assyria, tells the Assyrian version of the story of the great flood. The epic poem tells how the god Ea, disgusted by the evilness of the people of the city of Shuruppak, ordered the hero Utnapishtim to build a ship and to take on board his family and male and female pairs of all living creatures. The god then caused a flood to destroy all the bad people on earth. This story obviously shares the same origins as the biblical story of Noah's Ark.

The Bible today

The Bible is an all-time bestseller. It is probably one of the most widely read books in existence. It has been translated into more than 560 languages throughout the world. Many new translations are underway now. Missionaries often use the Bible as a basic text to teach people to read. Active Christians are encouraged to study the Bible every day. Among non-believers the Bible is seen as one of the greatest works of world literature and an important source of historical information about life in parts of the Middle East since very early times.

The illustration (below) shows the title page of the 1534 edition of the Bible translated into German by Martin Luther. Luther began the translation at the Wartburg castle while in hiding from the authorities of the Holy Roman Empire, who were outraged by his new ideas about religion.

Illuminated page of the Brother Haggadah codex (Barcelona, 1350). The Haggadah is a Jewish book with texts from the Torah, other literature, poems and rituals. Parts of the Haggadah are read or recited during the Jewish Passover supper.

The woodcut (below), by German Renaissance artist Albrecht Dürer, shows Saint Jerome, author of the most famous Latin translation of the Bible, as he removes a thorn from a lion's paw.

According to Christian tradition, the four books of the Gospels were written by Matthew, Mark, Luke and John. The first three were written between AD 70–80 and the latter around AD 100. The illustration (left), from a Byzantine Gospel, shows Matthew, Mark, Luke and John standing in front of a kind of visual summary of the episodes in their various books.

The Persian Empire

The tomb of King Cyrus still stands at Pasargadae, in modern Iran. The tomb, vandalized shortly after Cyrus's death, was restored by Alexander the Great, who greatly admired Cyrus.

The Jewish exile in Babylon ended in 539 BC when the mighty Babylonian Empire was defeated by the Persian king, Cyrus the Great. Cyrus was a descendant of an Indo-European people who moved into western Iran in about 1300 BC. The Persians, and their neighbours, the Medes, lived on the fringes of Babylonia until Cyrus became king in 559 BC. Cyrus's first move was to overthrow the Median Kingdom, which was ruled by his grandfather. He then attacked the Lydians in Asia Minor and finally, Babylon, to create the largest empire known until then. The Persian Empire lasted for 200 years, reaching its greatest extent under King Darius I (522–486 BC), when its frontiers stretched from Libya in the west to northern India in the east. The Persians were enlightened rulers. They allowed a measure of regional self-government and permitted exiles to return to their homelands. They also allowed religious freedom. Syria and Palestine were part of the Persian Empire and the Jews who had been exiled to Babylon were given the option of returning home. When the exiles returned to Jerusalem they found the city in ruins, its walls destroyed. Despite many difficulties, in 516 BC, under the prophets Haggahi and Zacariah, they rebuilt the Temple. In 458 BC the prophet Ezra returned with more exiles. Later, under the prophet Neemiah, the city walls were rebuilt, and social and religious life was reorganized. The era of Mesopotamian dominance in the the Middle East ended when the Persian Empire was overthrown in 333 BC by Alexander the Great.

The griffen was a common image in Persian art. Here it is represented on a silver drinking horn, called a rhyton, from about 400 BC.

The golden chariot drawn by four horses was part of a treasure of gold and silver objects and coins found at the River of Oxus. The Persians were skilled metalworkers and many beautiful objects are still in existence.

This baked clay cylinder, known as the Cyrus Cylinder, records how Cyrus conquered Babylon and how he restored the various gods to their home cities. It does not specifically refer to the Hebrews, as they were just one of many exiled populations that the king allowed to return home.

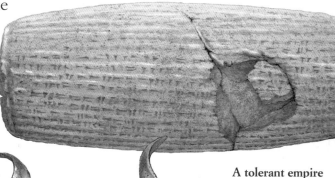

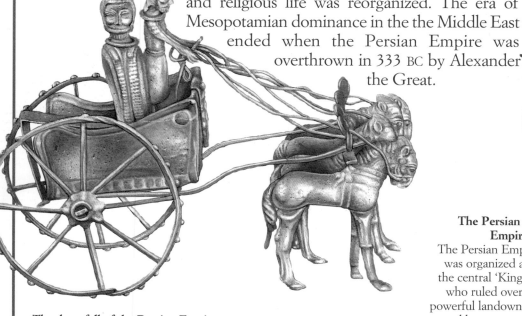

The downfall of the Persian Empire

The Greek military leader from Macedonia, called Alexander the Great, defeated the Persian king Darius III at the Battle of Issus in 333 BC. The following year he sent his general Parmenio to win Syria and Palestine. Alexander conquered a huge empire, even larger than the Persian one. He brought Greek culture to the Middle East; Greek customs, the Greek language, Greek money, cities and ideas predominated in the lands Alexander had conquered. Jerusalem, like other cities in the Middle East, was also Hellenized (which means adopting many of the customs of the Greek rulers).

The Persian Empire

The Persian Empire was organized around the central 'King of Kings' who ruled over a court of powerful landowners, priests and bureaucrats. The king controlled the army and appointed all the local governors and officials. The land was divided into provinces, called satrapies, each one ruled over by a Persian or local satrap. The king sent inspectors, known as the 'King's Ears' on tour all over the empire and they reported back to him continually. The provinces were well connected by good roads and trade flourished. The empire was financed by taxes paid by all the various peoples under Persian rule.

A tolerant empire

It is said that when King Cyrus entered Babylon the people spread green branches before him and hailed him as their true king. Cyrus was tolerant of all the religions of the peoples of his empire. He ordered that all the statues and treasures of gods that the Babylonian kings had accumulated be returned to their homelands. He also warned his soldiers not to treat the local populations harshly. Cyrus believed that if the conquered peoples could worship as they please then they would accept Persian rule more easily.

This silver deer dates from the 5th century BC. It comes from Persepolis.

Mithras slaying the sacrificial bull. The sacrifice of the bull was the most important ceremony in the Mithraic tradition.

Persian religion

By the time of Darius, the kings of Persia were all Zoroastrians. Zoroaster rejected the worship of all gods except one, called *Ahura Mazda*, meaning the 'Wise Lord'. The religion began some time in the 6th century BC. It had some influence on the Jewish and Christian religions. In pre-Zoroastrian times Mithras was the most important among many gods. Older religious beliefs persisted alongside Zoroastrianism for centuries. In the 2nd century AD Zoroastrianism became the state religion.

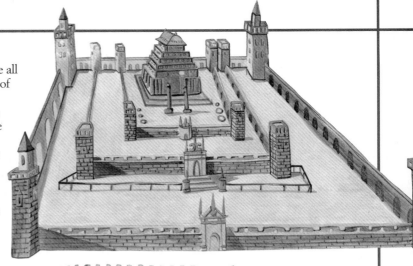

Rebuilding the Temple

Cyrus encouraged the reconstruction of the ancient temples of his empire. This was recorded by the Hebrews in the Bible in the following manner: '*This is what Cyrus King of Persia says: 'The Lord, the God of heaven, has given me all the kingdom of the earth and he has appointed me to build a temple for him at Jerusalem in Judah... go up to Jerusalem in Judah and build the temple of the Lord, the God of Israel...' Moreover, King Cyrus brought out all the articles belonging to the temple of the Lord, which Nebuchadrezzar had carried away from Jerusalem... Sheshbazzar brought all these along when the exiles came up from Babylon to Jerusalem*'. Ezra 1, 2–11.

This illustration from a Passover Haggadah drawn in Germany in the 18th century shows the Second Temple in Jerusalem.

The many Hebrews who stayed in Babylon or who lived outside Jerusalem built simple synagogues like the one shown here.

The Persians and the Greeks

The Persians were wary of the strong Classical Greek civilization on their western frontier. The Athenians had even dared to support an uprising against the Persians in Asia Minor in 498 BC. The Persians wanted to annex Greece to their empire. A great battle took place at Marathon in 490 BC, but the Greeks defeated their powerful neighbours. They beat them again in 480 BC at the Battle of Salamis, although not before the Persians had looted and burned Athens, destroying the buildings on the Acropolis, including the temple of the goddess Athena.

A Greek hoplite (soldier) in full military uniform.

The return from Exile

The Hebrews had been in Babylon for about fifty years. Those who returned to Jerusalem were either very old or the sons and daughters of those who had been exiled. It is not known exactly how many returned to Israel, but it was probably a minority of the Jewish population in Babylon. Most would have chosen to stay in Babylon. The several thousand who did return looked upon the journey as a kind of second Exodus. They were led by Sheshbazzar and Zerubbabel.

Under Darius a standing army was formed. At the core of the army were 'the ten thousand immortals', who were highly trained soldiers. The frieze (above) shows members of the Palace Guard at the Persian capital of Susa.

BLACK SEA

CASPIAN SEA

MEDITERRANEAN SEA

• Sardis   • Gordian

• Kabul

Taxila •

This doubled-head griffin is from the city of Persepolis.

• Antioch   • Nineveh

Ecbatana •

Sidon •   • Damascus
• Tyre

Persepolis

Ancient Persia was ruled from Susa (and, at times, Babylon and Ecbatana). But Darius I the Great built a magnificent city called Persepolis in a remote, mountainous area. The mixture of architectural and decorative styles used in the city reflect a blend of the many peoples and customs that composed the empire.

Memphis •

• Babylon   • Susa

Pasargadae •

Persepolis •

RED SEA

PERSIAN GULF

Greeks and Romans

After Alexander the Great's death his empire split into several parts. The Bible Lands were carved up between two of Alexander's generals: Ptolemy, based in Egypt, and Seleucus, based in Syria. At first the Ptolemies ruled Palestine, but they were soon ousted by the Seleucids. However, despite the wars among Alexander's heirs, the region was still dominated by Greek culture. Many Palestinian Jews, particularly rich city-dwellers, adopted Greek ways. But when the Seleucid ruler, Antiochus IV, prohibited Jewish religious practices, forcing the Jews to make sacrifices to Zeus, they revolted. Known as the Revolt of the Maccabees, it was led by a family of country priests, the Hasmonaeans. The Hasmonaeans freed Palestine from foreign rule, making it independent for the first time since the Babylonians destroyed the Temple in the 6th century BC. Palestine was greatly enlarged under the Hasmonaeans, but its independence was short lived. Across the Mediterranean, in Italy, the Romans were becoming more and more powerful. The Romans wanted Palestine under their control because the area was a buffer zone between themselves and their enemies the Parthians, who now controlled Mesopotamia. The Romans intervened to settle a civil war between descendants of the Hasmonaean kingdom. The Roman general Pompey entered Jerusalem in 63 BC. In 40 BC, the Romans appointed Herod king.

'So Alexander reigned twelve years and then died. And his servants bore rule every one in his place. And after his death they all put crowns upon themselves; so did their sons after them many years: and evils were multiplied on Earth'. 1 Maccabees 1, 7–9.

Coin showing Antiochus IV, the Seleucid king who tried to unify his kingdom by making all its citizens worship the Greek gods. This provoked the Revolt of the Maccabees and the beginning of the end for the Seleucid kingdom.

Pottery head of the Greek goddess Aphrodite, dating from the 3rd century BC, found at Dor in northern Palestine. After Alexander, the Middle East was ruled by Greeks and the Greek language and customs were widespread.

The Old Testament in Greek

After Alexander many new Greek-style towns sprang up in the Middle East. Alexandria, in Egypt, became one of the most important. There was a large Jewish community in Alexandria. Most of the Alexandrian Jews spoke Greek and did not know Hebrew. In order to teach Jewish laws and traditions, the Old Testament was translated into Greek. According to legend, the translation was done by 70 of Jerusalem's finest scholars and was completed in just 72 days. The famous translation, known as the Septuagint (Greek for seventy), has been used ever since by both Jewish and Christian scholars.

Pottery lamp from the Roman city of Caesarea.

Jewish scribe at work.

Herod the Great

Herod was born in about 73 BC. He was the son of Antipater, advisor to John Hyrcanus, the last member of the Hasmonaean family. Like his father, Herod was an able politician. He supported Rome throughout his life, making tactical switches in allegiance depending on how the wind blew in Rome. The Romans appreciated such a loyal follower and made him king over an increasingly large part of Palestine, or Judaea, as the Romans called the region. At home, Herod was an unpopular king. Many of his Jewish citizens hated him, not only for his close ties with Rome, but also because he was a repressive and often violent ruler.

One of Herod's most famous building projects was the reconstruction of the Temple in Jerusalem. Although not loved by his subjects the Jewish sages greatly admired his splendid Temple, saying 'He who has not seen Herod's building, has never seen a beautiful building'. Nothing remains of Herod's Temple today.

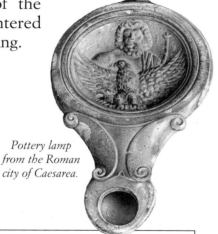

1. Herod's Temple
2. Antonia Fortress
3. The Western Wall (still standing today)
4. Meeting Hall
5. Court of the Gentiles
6. Viaduct

During the Roman period, Jewish burials were carried out in two separate stages. The dead person was first wrapped in a linen shroud and laid to rest in a family tomb. When the flesh had decayed, relatives gathered up the bones and placed them in a stone box, called an ossuary. Some ossuaries were plain, but others were very ornate.

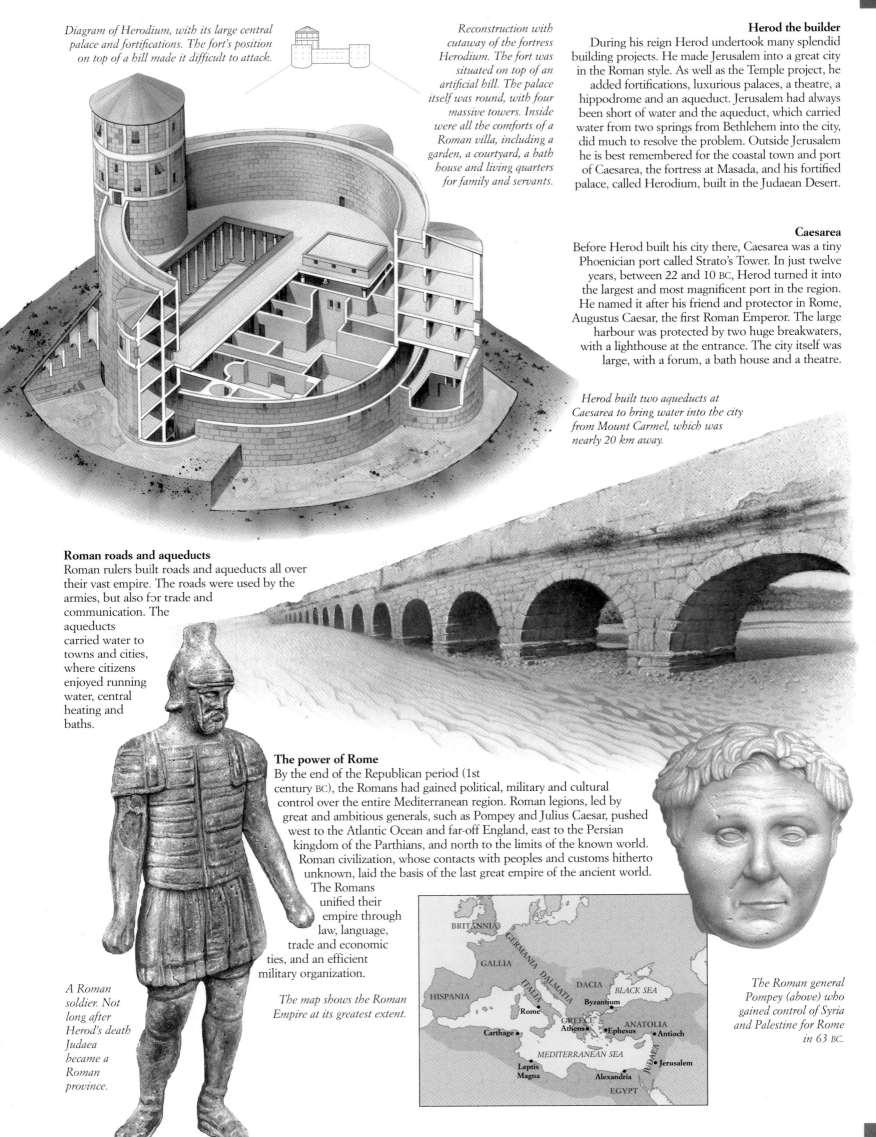

Diagram of Herodium, with its large central palace and fortifications. The fort's position on top of a hill made it difficult to attack.

Reconstruction with cutaway of the fortress Herodium. The fort was situated on top of an artificial hill. The palace itself was round, with four massive towers. Inside were all the comforts of a Roman villa, including a garden, a courtyard, a bath house and living quarters for family and servants.

Herod the builder

During his reign Herod undertook many splendid building projects. He made Jerusalem into a great city in the Roman style. As well as the Temple project, he added fortifications, luxurious palaces, a theatre, a hippodrome and an aqueduct. Jerusalem had always been short of water and the aqueduct, which carried water from two springs from Bethlehem into the city, did much to resolve the problem. Outside Jerusalem he is best remembered for the coastal town and port of Caesarea, the fortress at Masada, and his fortified palace, called Herodium, built in the Judaean Desert.

Caesarea

Before Herod built his city there, Caesarea was a tiny Phoenician port called Strato's Tower. In just twelve years, between 22 and 10 BC, Herod turned it into the largest and most magnificent port in the region. He named it after his friend and protector in Rome, Augustus Caesar, the first Roman Emperor. The large harbour was protected by two huge breakwaters, with a lighthouse at the entrance. The city itself was large, with a forum, a bath house and a theatre.

Herod built two aqueducts at Caesarea to bring water into the city from Mount Carmel, which was nearly 20 km away.

Roman roads and aqueducts

Roman rulers built roads and aqueducts all over their vast empire. The roads were used by the armies, but also for trade and communication. The aqueducts carried water to towns and cities, where citizens enjoyed running water, central heating and baths.

The power of Rome

By the end of the Republican period (1st century BC), the Romans had gained political, military and cultural control over the entire Mediterranean region. Roman legions, led by great and ambitious generals, such as Pompey and Julius Caesar, pushed west to the Atlantic Ocean and far-off England, east to the Persian kingdom of the Parthians, and north to the limits of the known world. Roman civilization, whose contacts with peoples and customs hitherto unknown, laid the basis of the last great empire of the ancient world.
The Romans unified their empire through law, language, trade and economic ties, and an efficient military organization.

A Roman soldier. Not long after Herod's death Judaea became a Roman province.

The map shows the Roman Empire at its greatest extent.

BRITANNIA
GERMANIA
GALLIA
HISPANIA
ITALIA
DALMATIA
DACIA
BLACK SEA
Byzantium
Rome
GREECE
Athens
ANATOLIA
Ephesus
Antioch
Carthage
MEDITERRANEAN SEA
JUDAEA
Jerusalem
Leptis Magna
Alexandria
EGYPT

The Roman general Pompey (above) who gained control of Syria and Palestine for Rome in 63 BC.

The Life of Jesus

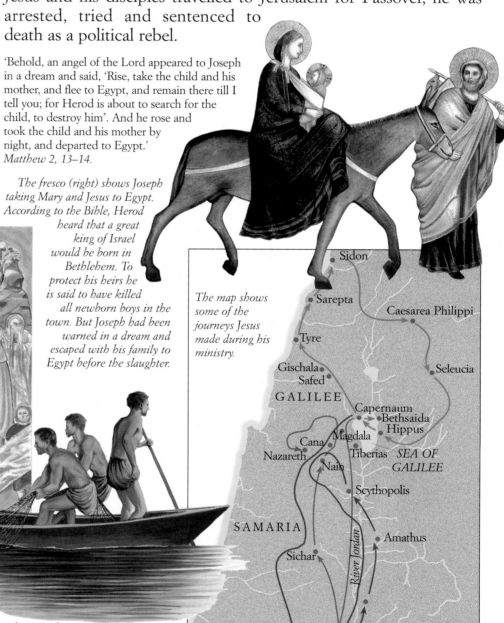

Most of what we know about the life of Jesus is based on the gospels, the first four books in the New Testament. But the gospels are not meant to be accurate biographies, and their version of Jesus's life is patchy and incomplete. Most scholars agree that Jesus was born in Bethlehem towards the end of Herod's reign, probably around 6–4 BC. He spent his youth in Nazareth, near the Sea of Galilee, where the family moved during the unrest that followed Herod's death. Jesus grew up in a Jewish family. As a young man he was baptized in the River Jordan by his cousin, John the Baptist. At about the age of 30 he began to preach, attracting disciples and a large following. He was loved by the common people because he preached against poverty and the hypocrisy of rich people and priests. He made enemies among both the Roman and Jewish authorities. When Jesus and his disciples travelled to Jerusalem for Passover, he was arrested, tried and sentenced to death as a political rebel.

Mosaic showing The Adoration of the Magi (*or* The Wise Men). *According to tradition, three kings from the East followed a miraculous guiding star to Bethlehem, where they paid homage to the baby Jesus. They brought gifts of gold, frankincense and myrrh. Christians around the world celebrate the birth of Christ every year at Christmas, on December 25.*

The ministry of Jesus in Galilee

Jesus began to preach near his home in Galilee. He taught all kinds of people, not just the men, but women and children, non-believers, the diseased and the outcast. He preached in synagogues, in the open air, on the lake shore and on the road. His message was simple and direct so that everyone could understand. He gathered the twelve disciples during this period. His ministry was quite brief, probably only lasting for about one year.

'Behold, an angel of the Lord appeared to Joseph in a dream and said, 'Rise, take the child and his mother, and flee to Egypt, and remain there till I tell you; for Herod is about to search for the child, to destroy him'. And he rose and took the child and his mother by night, and departed to Egypt.' *Matthew 2, 13–14.*

The fresco (right) shows Joseph taking Mary and Jesus to Egypt. According to the Bible, Herod heard that a great king of Israel would be born in Bethlehem. To protect his heirs he is said to have killed all newborn boys in the town. But Joseph had been warned in a dream and escaped with his family to Egypt before the slaughter.

The map shows some of the journeys Jesus made during his ministry.

Fishing was an important activity in Galilee, where Jesus began to preach. Four of his disciples – Andrew, Peter, James and John – were fishermen.

During his ministry Jesus is said to have performed many miracles, including healing the blind and the sick and raising the dead. A favourite story (left) tells how Jesus and his mother Mary were at a wedding in Cana when their hosts ran out of wine. Jesus turned jugs of water into wine. On another occasion (fresco, above) Jesus brought a man called Lazarus back to life after he had been dead for four days.

Mosaic showing another famous miracle: Jesus was preaching on the shores of the Sea of Galilee. He asked his disciples to feed the crowd. When they said they had only five loaves of bread and two fishes, he ordered them to feed the crowd anyway. As they distributed the loaves and fishes they were miraculously multiplied and everyone had enough to eat.

Miniature from the Irish Book of Kells, showing Jesus being arrested. It was painted about AD 800.

The entrance into Jerusalem

'The next day the great crowd that had come for the Feast heard that Jesus was on his way to Jerusalem. They took palm branches and went out to meet him, shouting, Hosanna!' John 12, 12–13.

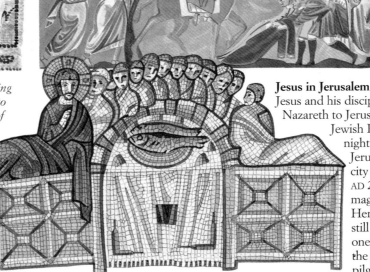

Jesus in Jerusalem

Jesus and his disciples travelled from Nazareth to Jerusalem to celebrate the Jewish Passover. They slept the night in Bethany, near Jerusalem, and entered the city the next day. It was about AD 26 and Jerusalem was a magnificent city with all of Herod's splendid buildings still in place. Passover was one of the major festivals, and the city was crowded with pilgrims. According to the gospels, Jesus preached on the Temple Mount. He also overturned the stalls of traders who were selling animals for sacrifice and exchanging coins for donation to the Temple. His activities displeased both the Roman and Jewish authorities.

Mosaic showing Christ and the disciples during the Last Supper, from Ravenna, Italy.

Arrest

Jesus was arrested after the Last Supper. He and his disciples were on their way back to Bethany for the night when they stopped off to pray in the Garden of Gethsemane on the Mount of Olives. One of the disciples, Judas Iscariot, had betrayed Jesus's whereabouts to the Roman soldiers.

Painting by Italian pre-Renaissance artist Simone Martini, showing Jesus on the Cross.

Jesus is flogged

The gospels recount that Jesus was flogged before the crucifixion. Some suggest that this was carried out as a warning by Pilate, who did not wish to crucify Jesus. Others say that it was normal practice to flog a man before crucifixion. Jesus was also mocked by the Roman soldiers before his death. They dressed him in a red (or purple) robe and placed a crown of thorns on his head (a parody of the crown of laurel leaves worn by Roman emperors).

This relief carving in bronze shows Jesus being flogged. It was made in the 11th or 12th century.

Trial and crucifixion

Jesus was questioned first by the High Priest, Caiaphas, about his actions in the Temple and his claims to be the Messiah. He was then tried by the Romans under the prefect, Pontius Pilate. He was judged to be a revolutionary and sentenced to death by crucifixion.

Resurrection

Christians believe that Jesus died on the Cross but that he was resurrected (brought back to life) after his death. He is said to have appeared to his disciples and other followers many times after his death and before he ascended to heaven.

Stone in the Church of the Holy Sepulchre in Jerusalem, on which an angel is said to have appeared to the women who came to anoint Jesus's body on the Sabbath after his death. The angel explained to them that the tomb was empty because Christ had risen.

Roman Rule

The 1st and 2nd centuries AD were turbulent times in Palestine. Tension between Romans and Jews was constant and twice exploded into full-scale war. The First Revolt broke out in AD 66. Although it lasted seven years, until the fall of Masada in AD 74, the Jews were already beaten by AD 70 when Jerusalem and the Second Temple were destroyed. Almost sixty years later, in AD 132, the Second Revolt erupted when the Roman Emperor Hadrian announced plans to refound Jerusalem as a Roman city, called Aelia Capitolina, and to build a temple to Jupiter on the site of the Second Temple. The Jewish rebels were led by Simeon Bar Kochba. It took the Romans three and a half years to put the rebellion down. A large number of Jews died during the revolt and many more emigrated. There were now regions and towns in Palestine with mixed populations and areas where non-Jews were a majority.

The first Emperor of the Roman empire, Augustus. The burden of Roman rule became more and more intolerable to the Jews

The Roman Emperor Hadrian whose activities in Jerusalem and ban on the practice of circumcision sparked Jewish wrath and the Second Revolt.

The fall of Masada

The dramatic events at Masada in AD 73 signalled the end of the First Revolt. The huge, flat-topped rock near the shores of the Dead Sea was a natural stronghold which had been further fortified by Herod. A Roman garrison when the war began, it was taken by Jewish Zealots in AD 66. They held out until the Romans built a massive siege ramp. Rather than be taken alive, the 960 Jews on Masada committed suicide during the night before the Romans arrived.

The First Revolt

The Jews had always resented the Roman presence in Palestine. The actions of a series of corrupt and incompetent Roman procurators in the period leading up to the Revolt triggered it off. At first the Jews were led by high-ranking priests, such as Josephus. Later, they split into factions, weakening their cause by fighting among themselves. Vespasian and his son, Titus, led the Romans.

The Arch of Titus, built in AD 81, had a panel with a relief carving showing Roman soldiers parading the seven-branched ritual candlestick and other treasure from the Second Temple in Jerusalem through the streets of Rome.

Arrowheads found on Masada dating from the time of the siege.

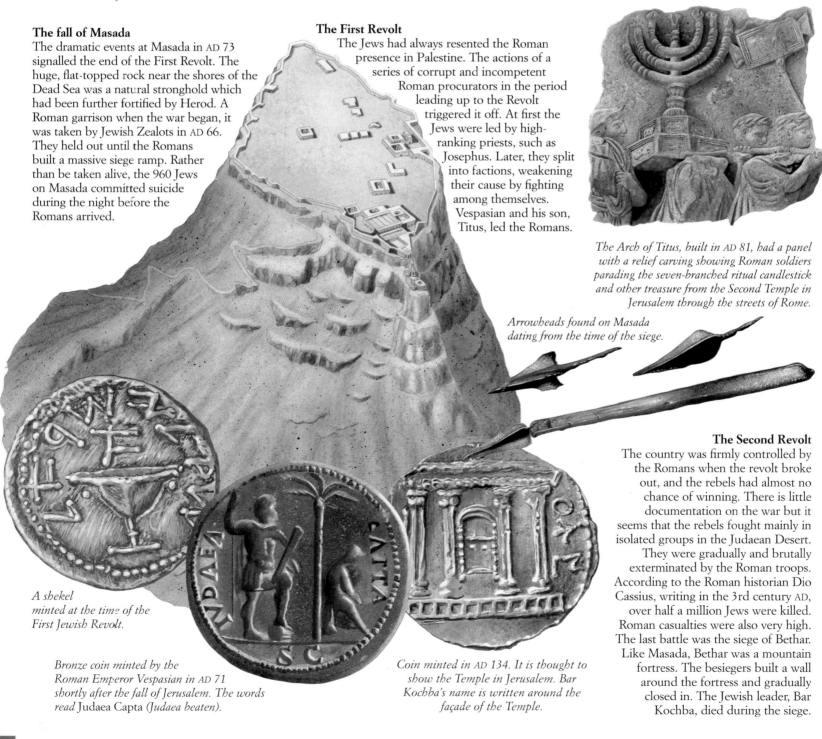

A shekel minted at the time of the First Jewish Revolt.

Bronze coin minted by the Roman Emperor Vespasian in AD 71 shortly after the fall of Jerusalem. The words read Judaea Capta (Judaea beaten).

Coin minted in AD 134. It is thought to show the Temple in Jerusalem. Bar Kochba's name is written around the façade of the Temple.

The Second Revolt

The country was firmly controlled by the Romans when the revolt broke out, and the rebels had almost no chance of winning. There is little documentation on the war but it seems that the rebels fought mainly in isolated groups in the Judaean Desert. They were gradually and brutally exterminated by the Roman troops. According to the Roman historian Dio Cassius, writing in the 3rd century AD, over half a million Jews were killed. Roman casualties were also very high. The last battle was the siege of Bethar. Like Masada, Bethar was a mountain fortress. The besiegers built a wall around the fortress and gradually closed in. The Jewish leader, Bar Kochba, died during the siege.

Sleeping quarters

Inside courtyard

Ovens

Sandal and fish hook from the 1st century AD.

Jewish house from about the 3rd century AD. This large building would have belonged to a wealthy family.

Main dining and living area.

Oven

Storeroom

Daily life

In the early Christian era the Jews of Palestine continued to live mainly in country villages, earning their livings as farmers. Fishing was an important activity in the northern part of the region. The Jewish calendar, with important dates for each year, was proclaimed by the Sanhedrin (Jewish council) from Jerusalem.

The synagogue

Synagogues had existed since the Exile in Babylon, but it was only after the destruction of the Second Temple that they became places of prayer. The synagogue was also the centre of the Jewish community. After the 4th century BC the Romans began to prohibit the building of new synagogues and in some cases even destroyed existing ones.

Reconstruction of a synagogue.

1.
2.
3.
4.
5.
6.
7.

Tools and utensils dating from the time of the Second Revolt. 1. Bronze vessel; 2.Basket made of palm; 3. Knife; 4. Key; 5. Wooden bowls and spoon; 6. Mirror; 7. Glass bowls.

Limestone slab with a warning in Greek prohibiting the entry of non-Jews to the Temple. It dates from the time of the Second Temple.

Catacombs

Jews were forbidden entry to Jerusalem after the destruction of the Second Temple. After that time the town of Bet She'arim became an important centre, particularly for Jews outside Palestine who wished to be buried in the Holy Land. Long underground corridors and chambers filled with Jewish tombs have been found in the area around the synagogue.

View of the catacombs with Jewish tombs at Bet She'arim.

Early Christianity

According to the Bible (Acts 1, 15), after Christ's death the believers were only about 120 people. The beginning of the Christian Church is traditionally dated to the Pentecost after Christ died. On that day his followers were gathered together and were exalted by an intense religious experience. *'They saw what seemed to be tongues of fire that separated and came to rest on each of them. All of them were filled with the Holy Spirit...'* Acts 2, 3–4. Their leader, Peter, preached the first Christian sermon, saying that Jesus, who had been crucified and had risen again, was both 'Lord and Christ'. He told them to believe in Jesus, to ask forgiveness for their sins and to be baptised as Christians. According to Acts, 3,000 new converts were made on that day alone. Thereafter Christianity spread quickly – within 300 years the new faith was common throughout most of the ancient world and had become the officially sponsored religion of the vast Roman Empire.

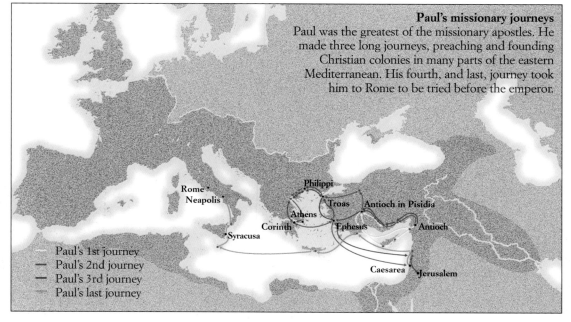

Peter (left) and Paul (right) from a child's tombstone of the 4th century AD. Peter and Paul were of fundamental importance in spreading the Christian religion after Christ's death.

Mosaic from Ravenna in Italy showing the four gospels – Matthew, Mark, Luke and John – in a cupboard.

Paul's missionary journeys
Paul was the greatest of the missionary apostles. He made three long journeys, preaching and founding Christian colonies in many parts of the eastern Mediterranean. His fourth, and last, journey took him to Rome to be tried before the emperor.

Rome
Neapolis
Philippi
Troas
Athens
Antioch in Pisidia
Corinth
Ephesus
Antioch
Syracusa
Caesarea
Jerusalem

— Paul's 1st journey
— Paul's 2nd journey
— Paul's 3rd journey
— Paul's last journey

Painting showing the martyrdom of Saint Paul. After long years of travelling Paul returned to Jerusalem where he was arrested. As a Roman citizen he was allowed to be tried before the Emperor in Rome. He made the long journey to Rome partly by boat and partly on foot. Paul lived under house arrest in Rome for several years. During that time he preached and continued to write to the Christian communities he had founded. According to tradition, he was executed in Rome in AD 67.

Peter and the early church
Peter led the church in Jerusalem for about 15 years after the death of Jesus. By tradition, his name is associated with Rome where he is said to have lived for 25 years. He was the first pope. His tomb is thought to be buried deep in the foundations of St. Peter's Church in Rome.

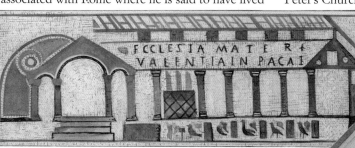

Mosaic of an early Christian basilica built in the Roman style.

Reconstruction of the House of Peter at Capernaum.

Assembly hall

Early churches
Early Christians met in each other's houses rather than in churches. In fact, at that time the word 'church' referred to the people (or congregation) rather than a building. From the time of Constantine the Great, the first Christian emperor, conditions for Christians improved and churches began to be built.

Christian martyrs
Christianity emerged in Palestine and spread throughout the Mediterranean and beyond when these areas were under Roman rule. Because Christians refused to take part in traditional Roman religion they were persecuted. Many were executed for their beliefs. Persecution and killings were periodic and tended to coincide with difficult local conditions. For example, a bad harvest which caused famine might be blamed on local Christians who were then punished.

Christianity and the Roman Empire

Early in the 4th century AD the Roman Emperor, Constantine the Great, accepted Christianity and encouraged it to spread even further among his subjects. Constantine moved the centre of the Empire from Rome to Constantinople (previously Byzantium, but renamed Constantinople in the Emperor's honour). Christianity and empire were closely linked; as the Church grew it modelled its structure on the empire. Despite setbacks, by about AD 600 most of the area the Roman Empire had covered was largely Christian.

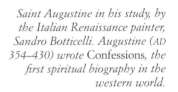

In AD 325 Constantine sent his mother Helen to Jerusalem to identify the places where Jesus had lived. This painting shows Constantine (left) and his mother (centre) just before she set out on her journey.

Byzantine Jerusalem reached its zenith under the emperor Justinian (right) and his wife, Theodora, who reigned AD 527–65.

Saint Augustine in his study, by the Italian Renaissance painter, Sandro Botticelli. Augustine (AD 354–430) wrote Confessions, *the first spiritual biography in the western world.*

Early Christians meet in the catacombs around Rome (below). The catacombs were underground burial places. The Christians also used them to meet in secret during times of persecution.

Christianity and other religions

Christians despised other religions. The many forms of paganism that were widespread in the Roman Empire – the eastern cults of Isis, Attis and Mithras, and the classical cults of Greece and Rome – were regarded as evil. Even so, Christianity absorbed many influences from these groups. For example, sun worship was common in the 3rd century; soon afterwards the Christian Church adopted the Winter Solstice, 25 December, as the date of Christ's birth.

Jews, Gentiles and Christians

The first Christians were Jews who followed both Jewish law and Christ's teachings. At first they did not try to convert gentiles (non-Jews), although more and more joined the movement. At the Council of Jerusalem in AD 49 it was agreed that gentiles did not have to obey strict Jewish law (including circumcision and dietary restrictions) to become Christians. Gradually Christianity became the religion of gentiles and orthodox Jews rejected it.

Splits in the Church

The Christian Church split early into an Eastern Church, based in Constantinople and a Western Church, based in Rome. Other Christian groups, such as the Copts in Egypt, had formed even earlier. Many of these divisions have survived to the present day.

Coptic icon, showing Christ with his hand on an abbot's shoulder.

Moses

Moses was a Hebrew prophet and leader. The son of Jewish parents, he was raised by an Egyptian princess in the pharaoh's court as a prince. When Moses found out he was a Hebrew he began to protect the Jewish slaves, eventually leading them out of Egypt to freedom (see pp. 20–21). In the Bible, Moses is the person God chose as his representative to make his covenant with the Hebrew people.

Eve

According to the Bible, Eve was the mother of all humanity. She and Adam, the first man, were tricked by the serpent into committing the original sin, for which they were expelled from the Garden of Eden. For believers, this is the origin of all mankind's troubles. In her various forms and under many different names, Eve has been a symbol of mother- and womanhood across many cultures.

Adam

According to the Bible, Adam was the first man, and the high point of God's creation. Together with Eve, he was to rule over the Garden of Eden. Adam is said to have given names to all God's creatures.

David

The second King of Israel (after Saul), David ruled for about forty years over a united country with its capital at Jerusalem. Jesus is said to be descended from the same family. An accomplished poet and musician, and a skilful warrior, it is thought that David was the author of the Old Testament Book of Psalms. As a boy he fought and defeated the giant Goliath, becoming a lasting symbol of courage and faith.

Daniel

This Old Testament prophet is best known for his adventure in the lions' den. The lions did not savage him because he was protected by God.

Judith

The beautiful Jewish widow, Judith, is the heroine of the Old Testament Book of Judith (considered apocryphal by Protestants). According to the Bible, when Nebuchadrezzar, King of Assyria (in reality, King of Babylon), sent his general Holofernes to attack her city in Judah, Judith cut off his head and saved the city.

Jonah

Jonah is one of the Minor Prophets in the Old Testament. He is famous for being swallowed by a whale while trying to escape from God. He then went to the city of Nineveh and saved its inhabitants by preaching against their wickedness.

People of the Bible

Stories from the lives of many people are told in the Bible. We now know that some biblical characters, such as King David, and Jesus and the disciples, were real people, although we can't always be sure that they lived their lives exactly as it is told in the Bible. Other characters, such as Eve or Noah, are much more difficult to place in history, and most people now think that they were in legends that were meant to explain and give meaning to our origins. Whether or not they existed in real life, the characters in the Bible have been very important in Western civilization. They have had a strong and lasting influence in art, literature, philosophy and science. Because the Bible is also a sacred book for Muslims, many biblical characters also appear in Islamic texts and art.

The Virgin Mary
As the mother of Jesus, Mary plays a supporting role in the New Testament. However, her importance grew in the centuries after Christ's death as people came to believe in the Virgin Birth. Mary is now a hugely popular figure in many Roman Catholic countries. People believe that she can help them to win God's favour. Pilgrimages and special ceremonies are carried out in her honour.

Jesus Christ
Christians believe that Christ is the Son of God, and the Messiah, who came to earth as a man to free people from their sins and to lead them to salvation. His life and works are recounted in the New Testament. He is the central figure in the Christian religion.

Jesus and the Samaritan woman
The Gospel of John tells how Jesus met a Samaritan woman at a well. He asked her for water, which was a scandalous act in those times. Jews and Samaritans were bitter enemies; also, rabbis did not speak to women in public. The unnamed woman was the first person in Samaria to believe that Jesus was the Messiah.

The Deposition
The word 'deposition' means the taking down of Christ's body from the cross. Four women are shown here: Christ's mother, Mary; her sister, Elizabeth; Mary Magdalene; and the Apostle James's mother, also called Mary.

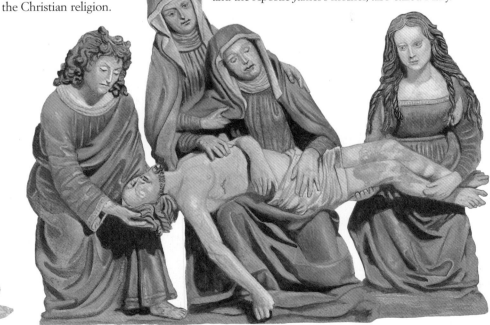

Above right, from the top

Saint Peter
Peter was a fisherman from the Sea of Galilee before becoming a disciple. His original name was Simon, but Jesus called him Peter (meaning 'rock'). He was the leader of the disciples and the early Christian community in Jerusalem. The Roman Catholic Church recognizes him as the first Pope. According to tradition, he died a martyr in Rome during the persecutions by the Emperor Nero. He is usually shown or represented by keys, symbolizing the power of the Church to forgive sin and open the way to eternal life.

Saint Paul
Saul of Tarsus, as Paul was known before he became a disciple, was a Jewish rabbi with a formal Greek education. At first he was a bitter enemy of Christianity, but after his conversion he became an outstanding figure in the early Church. He was largely responsible for spreading Christianity, helping it to become a world religion.

Saint Stephen
Stephen was the first Christian martyr. He was stoned to death by the Jews for prophesying the destruction of the Temple in Jerusalem and rejecting the laws of Moses.

Mary Magdalene
According to tradition, Mary was a prostitute saved by Jesus. She was present when Christ was crucified and was the first to speak to him after his resurrection.

The Age of Islam

Together with much of the rest of the Middle East, the Holy Land fell to Muslim control shortly after Muhammad's death in AD 632. The Christian Patriarch, Sophronius, surrendered the city of Jerusalem to the second Muslim Caliph, Omar, in AD 638. The Muslims were generally tolerant of the beliefs of the peoples they ruled over, particularly of the Jews and Christians because of their shared spiritual heritage – Muslims also recognise the Bible and its prophets as holy. Jews and Christians lived in their own separate communities, called *millets*, under their own laws. Pilgrims continued to come to the Holy Land and were allowed to visit sacred places.

Initially the Islamic world was united, but it soon split into several factions. Not all the factions were tolerant. During the 11th century, Caliph al-Hakim ordered the destruction of the Holy Sepulchre in Jerusalem. Also during the 11th century, the Seljuk Turks overran Turkey, threatening the Christian city of Constantinople.

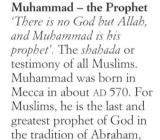

The ceramic tile (above) means Allah (the only god). Allah is just one of ninety-nine Arab names for God.

Muhammad – the Prophet
'There is no God but Allah, and Muhammad is his prophet'. The shahada or testimony of all Muslims. Muhammad was born in Mecca in about AD 570. For Muslims, he is the last and greatest prophet of God in the tradition of Abraham, Moses and Jesus.

The mosque
The mosque is the centre of religious life throughout the Muslim world. The model for mosques was based on a simple Arab city house of sun-dried bricks, and probably reproduced the plan of Muhammad's house in Medina.

The illustration (right) shows the faithful building the first mosque. It comes from a Turkish manuscript.

The miniature (below) shows Muhammad preaching to the faithful at Medina.

The call to prayer
Inside the mosque, prayers were guided by the *imam*, while from the minaret outside the mosque, the *muezzin* called the faithful to prayer five times each day.

Arabic culture
While Europe stagnated in the early Middle Ages, learning and technological advances went ahead in the Arab world. The Arabic language became an international language of science, literature and commerce.

Camels
Caravans of hundreds of camels carried not only goods but also the word of Islam along the vast Arabian trade routes, helping to spread the religion far and wide.

Travel by camel was the most practical way of crossing the arid desert zones of Arabia and the Middle East.

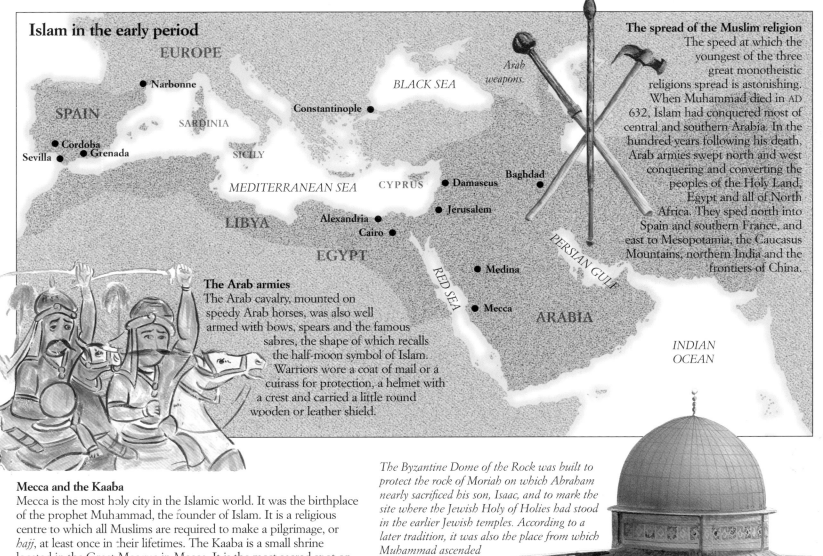

Islam in the early period

EUROPE

SPAIN

Narbonne

Cordoba
Sevilla • • Grenada

SARDINIA

Constantinople

BLACK SEA

Arab weapons.

SICILY

MEDITERRANEAN SEA

CYPRUS

Damascus

Baghdad

LIBYA

Alexandria
Cairo

Jerusalem

EGYPT

RED SEA

PERSIAN GULF

Medina

Mecca

ARABIA

INDIAN OCEAN

The spread of the Muslim religion
The speed at which the youngest of the three great monotheistic religions spread is astonishing. When Muhammad died in AD 632, Islam had conquered most of central and southern Arabia. In the hundred years following his death, Arab armies swept north and west conquering and converting the peoples of the Holy Land, Egypt and all of North Africa. They sped north into Spain and southern France, and east to Mesopotamia, the Caucasus Mountains, northern India and the frontiers of China.

The Arab armies
The Arab cavalry, mounted on speedy Arab horses, was also well armed with bows, spears and the famous sabres, the shape of which recalls the half-moon symbol of Islam. Warriors wore a coat of mail or a cuirass for protection, a helmet with a crest and carried a little round wooden or leather shield.

Mecca and the Kaaba
Mecca is the most holy city in the Islamic world. It was the birthplace of the prophet Muhammad, the founder of Islam. It is a religious centre to which all Muslims are required to make a pilgrimage, or *hajj*, at least once in their lifetimes. The Kaaba is a small shrine located in the Great Mosque in Mecca. It is the most sacred spot on earth for Muslims. The cube-shaped structure is covered with a black brocade cloth for most of the year. According to tradition, it was built by Abraham and then rebuilt after the flood by Ishmael, the forefather of the Arab peoples. In pre-Islamic times the Kaaba was filled with pagan idols (which Muhammad destroyed).

The Byzantine Dome of the Rock was built to protect the rock of Moriah on which Abraham nearly sacrificed his son, Isaac, and to mark the site where the Jewish Holy of Holies had stood in the earlier Jewish temples. According to a later tradition, it was also the place from which Muhammad ascended to heaven.

Jerusalem and Islam
Jerusalem is considered a Holy City of Islam. Early in his mission Muhammad told his followers to pray in the direction of Jerusalem. After his difficulties with the Jews of Medina, he changed the direction to Mecca. In the 7th century, Abd al-Malik built a large wooden mosque, which could hold up to 3,000 people, on the southern part of the Temple Mount. The beautiful Dome of the Rock was finished by AD 705. It was the first major Islamic sanctuary.

The tile (left) shows the Kaaba and the shahada *(testimony of all Muslims). It comes from the tomb of Muhammad.*

The miniature (below) shows pilgrims entering the Church of the Holy Sepulchre in Jerusalem. The church is guarded by Saracen soldiers.

Christian pilgrims
Pilgrimage was generally tolerated, with the exception of certain periods, for example, between 1009–1013, when the Caliph al-Hakim ordered the demolition of churches and synagogues. Biblical sites were also sacred for Muslims. Muslim rulers benefitted from the money the pilgrims paid to see the sites.

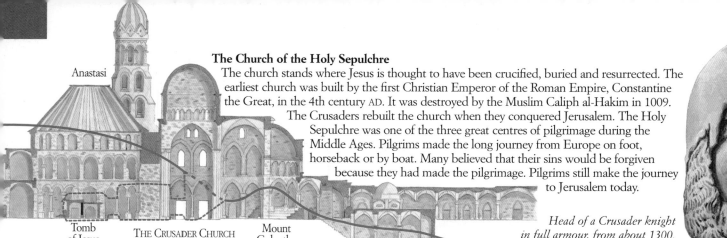

The Church of the Holy Sepulchre
The church stands where Jesus is thought to have been crucified, buried and resurrected. The earliest church was built by the first Christian Emperor of the Roman Empire, Constantine the Great, in the 4th century AD. It was destroyed by the Muslim Caliph al-Hakim in 1009. The Crusaders rebuilt the church when they conquered Jerusalem. The Holy Sepulchre was one of the three great centres of pilgrimage during the Middle Ages. Pilgrims made the long journey from Europe on foot, horseback or by boat. Many believed that their sins would be forgiven because they had made the pilgrimage. Pilgrims still make the journey to Jerusalem today.

Anastasi

Tomb of Jesus | THE CRUSADER CHURCH | Mount Golgotha

Head of a Crusader knight in full armour, from about 1300.

Crusaders and Pilgrims

During the 11th–13th centuries AD the Bible Lands were invaded many times by armies from Europe who tried to win Jerusalem back from its Muslim rulers. These invasions are known as the 'Crusades'. There were about eight Crusades in all. The first five were organized by the Pope, head of the Catholic Church in Rome. Pope Urban II called for the First Crusade in 1095. The Crusaders entered Jerusalem in 1099. They brutally murdered the city's inhabitants, hacking Muslims and Jews to death with their swords. The Arab leader Saladin recaptured Jersusalem in 1187, but the crusades and the fighting continued for another century or so, until the Christian armies were finally driven from the Holy Land. However, Europeans had been travelling to the Holy Land long before the Crusades began. As Christianity spread throughout Europe during the Middle Ages, increasing numbers of Christians went to Jerusalem to honour the site of Christ's death and resurrection and to be forgiven for their sins. These travellers are known as pilgrims.

Model of the ship that King Louis IX of France (Saint Louis) used during one of the last Crusades.

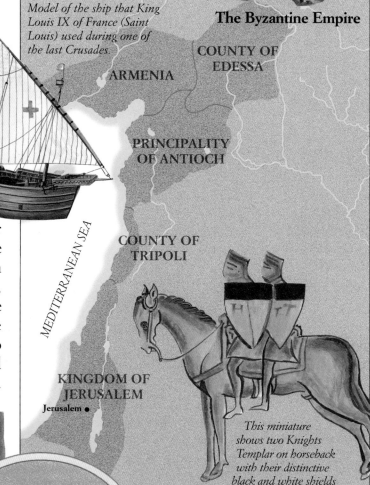

The Byzantine Empire

ARMENIA

COUNTY OF EDESSA

PRINCIPALITY OF ANTIOCH

MEDITERRANEAN SEA

COUNTY OF TRIPOLI

KINGDOM OF JERUSALEM
Jerusalem •

This miniature shows two Knights Templar on horseback with their distinctive black and white shields with a red cross.

ASIA | Noah's Ark

The Jordan

Iceland | Ireland

Great Britain | ✝ Jerusalem

Rome ○

MEDITERRANEAN SEA

PALESTINE

EUROPE

AFRICA

The map (left) places Jerusalem at the centre of the world. It also divides Europe from Asia.

Jerusalem at the centre of the world
During the Middle Ages a new kind of map appeared. Instead of the scientific and fairly accurate maps drawn in earlier times, these new ones, called *mappaemundi*, showed Jerusalem at the centre of the world. Other important religious sites were also shown. The maps were drawn by monks who wanted to show that the Holy Land was of utmost importance. During Crusader times and afterwards many circular maps of Jerusalem were drawn (like the one shown here, left). These were probably intended for use by pilgrims. They were quite detailed and practical – note the label *cambuum monete* (money changer), centre left.

The illuminated letter (right) comes from a 13th century History of the Crusades. *It shows the French King of Jerusalem, Baldwin IV defeating Saladin King of Egypt at Ashkelon in 1177.*

The castle Krak des Chevaliers was built by the Count of Tripoli. He sold it to the Order of the Knights Hospitalers who turned it into a sort of military monastery.

The beautiful Church of Saint Anne in Jerusalem dates from Crusader times. When the Islamic leader Saladin reconquered Jerusalem, he turned the church into a Koranic school.

Medieval miniature showing the siege of Antioch. The Christian principality of Antioch, conquered from the Muslims during the First Crusade, existed for 200 years.

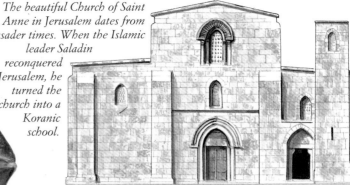

Crusader castles

During their stay in the Holy Land, the Crusaders filled the countryside with European-style churches, forts, castles and monasteries. Each Crusader warlord built his castle as a symbol of his power and control over a certain territory, just as he would have done in Europe. The castles were very expensive and most were soon sold to the military Orders of the Templars and Hospitalers, who turned them into military strongholds to defend the Christian kingdoms in the Holy Land.

The Crusader Orders

The Knights Templar was the first Crusader Order. It was founded by Hugh de Payns as a group of fighting monks who defended pilgrims on the road to Jerusalem. The Knights Hospitalers (or Knights of St John) was the other large Order. It was originally founded to care for the sick, but soon became a military Order.

This beautifully decorated glass goblet found in Syria dates to Crusader times. It is known as Charlemagne's cup. For a long time it was thought that the great medieval king had visited the Holy Land, although he never did.

The labyrinth (left) was a common symbol of pilgrimage. It is sculpted into the façades of many churches and houses along pilgrim routes.

These crosses, scratched into the wall in the Church of the Holy Sepulchre by the Crusaders, are still visible today.

Christians and Jews

On their journey to the Holy Land the first Crusaders massacred many Jews. The Christians saw the Jewish people as the impure murderers of Christ whose burial place they were going to liberate. Massacres of Jewish people continued in the following centuries. From about 1300 onwards the Jewish inhabitants of many European cities were expelled, burnt at the stake or sent to prison.

Massacre of Jews, from a 15th-century miniature.

The Tombs of the Just (below) – Joseph in Shechem, Rabbi Akiva in Tiberias and many others, were places that Jewish pilgrims visited.

Pilgrims in the Middle Ages travelled to many destinations, including places with relics of Christ's life. The relic above, from Assisi in Italy, is said to contain a thorn from the crown Christ wore when he was crucified.

Jewish pilgrims

The Christian presence and improved sea travel to the Holy Land encouraged Jewish pilgrims from Europe and elsewhere to make the journey to the land of their ancestors. Increasing numbers of Jews made the *aliyah* ('ascent') to Israel in the 13th century and some, from Yemen, North Africa and France, decided to settle in Jerusalem. Jewish pilgrims and a steady trickle of settlers continued to arrive in Israel in the centuries that followed.

Mamelukes and Ottomans

When Saladin came to power in Egypt in 1169 he followed the Muslim tradition of including a component of slave soldiers, or 'mamelukes', in his army. Mameluke is derived from an Arabic word for slave. Just eighty years later, Mameluke generals murdered one of Saladin's descendants as he was about to take power and established their own dynasty. The early Mamelukes were strong and able rulers. They expelled the last of the Crusaders from the Holy Land and rebuilt the economy in Egypt and Syria (at this time Jerusalem and the rest of Israel were part of an area called Syria). The Mamelukes ruled over Egypt and Syria until 1517 when they were defeated by Turkish tribes known as the Ottomans. The Ottomans were based in Anatolia (Turkey), where Osman founded the dynasty around 1300. Under Osman and his successors nearly all of Anatolia was conquered. The Ottoman Empire continued to expand until the 17th century. It began to decline after that time, although it continued to exist until 1922.

'Recite in the name of thy Lord who created all things, who created man from clots of blood'. In the Islamic tradition, with these words the Angel Gabriel encouraged Muhammad to speak out. The word for 'recitation' is qur'an (koran), which became the name for the collected revelations Allah gave to Muhammad. Gathered together in written form they are the basis of Islam. This miniature was painted in Syria during the Mameluke period.

The Hagia Sophia in Constantinople (modern Istanbul) was an ancient Christian church until it was converted into a mosque in 1453. It is now a museum.

Before the Ottomans invasions and wars among Latin peoples, Byzantines, Muslims, and Mongols had destroyed the former empires and political unity in the Middle East.

The Janissaries

The Janissaries were an elite troop of very highly trained Ottoman soldiers. Surprisingly, the Janissaries were not born as Muslims but were drafted from among the Christian population of the Balkans. The boys were taken while still young and converted to Islam. They were then given a long period of rigorous training. They had to obey very strict rules and were not allowed to marry. During the 15th and 16th centuries the Janissaries became a powerful political force. They were eliminated in 1826, during the so-called Auspicious Incident. When the Sultan Mahmud II wanted to modernize the army the Janissaries revolted. The Sultan responded by killing almost all of them.

The fall of Constantinople

The first Christian Emperor of the Roman Empire, Constantine the Great, founded Constantinople in the 4th century AD as the new Rome. The city became one of the great cities of the world, a centre of power, religion and wealth. As the capital of the Byzantine Empire, it was a Christian city, organized along Roman lines, but with Greek overtones given by the language and culture. The city was a glittering prize; the Ottomans tried many times to take it. They finally succeeded in 1453.

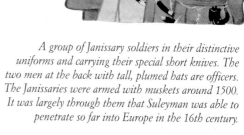

A group of Janissary soldiers in their distinctive uniforms and carrying their special short knives. The two men at the back with tall, plumed hats are officers. The Janissaries were armed with muskets around 1500. It was largely through them that Suleyman was able to penetrate so far into Europe in the 16th century.

The Mongols (left) were nomadic peoples from far-off Asia. The greatest land empire in world history was conquered by the Mongol leader Genghis Khan.

The power and prestige of the Ottoman Empire was greatly increased in 1520 when the Sultan Selim conquered the Mamelukes and acquired the holy places of Judaism, Christianity and Islam. These illustrations show the Muslim prophet Muhammad (left) and the most holy shrine in Islam, the Kaaba in Medina.

Islamic astronomers used astrolabes like this one to calculate the position of the sun and other stars with respect to the horizon. Astrolabes first appeared in Europe and the Islamic world about the 6th century AD. They were widely used throughout the Middle Ages. By the mid-15th century they were used by sailors to help them navigate.

Islam and science

The Islamic world made many important contributions to the development of science. They translated and then developed Greek and Byzantium scientific thought after the decline of those civilizations. Mathematics, astronomy, medicine, alchemy and mechanics were just some of the fields they worked in.

Dervish dancer. The Dervishes are a mystical offshoot of the Muslim religion.

Suleyman the Magnificent's flourishing signature.

Suleyman the Magnificent (1494/5–1566)

The Ottoman Sultan Suleyman the Magnificent undertook many bold military actions and extended the frontiers of the Empire greatly. His armies overtook the Balkans and moved far into the Hapsburg Empire in Europe. Suleyman surrounded himself with able administrators and statesmen and was able to rule very successfully. During his time he developed the Ottoman Empire in many fields beyond war. Law, literature, art and architecture all flourished during his reign. He was largely responsible for rebuilding Constantinople and other important cities, including Mecca and Baghdad, and transforming them into Muslim cities.

Aleppo

The city of Aleppo became one of the great Islamic cities in the Holy Land. Established by the Hittites many centuries before Islam, it was occupied by Islamic armies in AD 636. For the next thousand years it was fought over by the various powers in the Holy Land. Its citadel was built on a mound in the centre of the city. It was one of the strongest fortresses in the world.

This beautiful 16th century miniature comes from an Arab travel book. It gives a very detailed view of the citadel of Aleppo.

The Ottoman navy was very strong under Suleyman. The admiral Khar ad-Din (known in the West as Barbarossa, won a great battle against Venice and Spain in 1538 which gave the Ottomans virtual control of the Mediterranean. Barbarossa is shown here (left), peacefully sniffing a flower.

The end of the Ottoman Empire

During the 19th century the Empire began to lose many of its territories. In 1878 it was forced to give up Romania, Serbia, Montenegro, Bulgaria, Cyprus and other territories. In the 20th century the Turks themselves revolted against their rulers. In 1922 the last Ottoman Emperor, Mehmed IV Vahideddin, was overthrown and the modern state of Turkey was founded.

Lawrence of Arabia, an Englishman who helped Arabs in Egypt and Sudan free themselves from Ottoman rule.

Jerusalem

Jerusalem is one of the world's holiest cities. It is sacred to the peoples of the three great monotheistic religions – Jews, Christians and Muslims. It is also one of the oldest cities in the world. Traces of the earliest human settlement date to over 5,000 years ago. The city was known as Urusalim or Jebus until King David chose to make it the capital of the newly united nation of Israel in about 1000 BC. David brought the Ark of the Covenant to the city and his son Solomon built the First Temple there. Jerusalem has been the spiritual centre of Judaism ever since. At the beginning of the Christian era, Jesus was tried and crucified in the city. It is one of the holiest places in the world for Christians. In the Muslim tradition, the Temple Mount is the place from which the prophet Muhammad ascended to the heavens, to take his place alongside Allah. Jerusalem has been the third holiest city (after Mecca and Medina) for Muslims since the Arab conquest in AD 638. Arab Muslims do not call the city Jerusalem. For them it is al-Quds, meaning 'the Holy'. The city has been conquered and changed hands many times over the centuries. Each new conquerer and all the various religions have left traces of their presence. The Old City today is divided into four quarters – Jewish, Christian, Muslim and Armenian, reflecting the ethnic and religious composition of the city today.

Every age and every new conquest has left traces of itself in the city's appearance. This fragment of decoration was found near the Western Wall.

This sculpture shows Nehemiah directing the rebuilding of Jerusalem when the Jews returned to their homeland after the Babylonian exile.

Entrance to the Church of the Holy Sepulchre (left). The entrance dates from the time of the Crusades.

The medieval illuminated manuscript (above) shows the Holy City with the Dome of the Rock (right) and the Church of the Holy Sepulchre (left).

The Madaba Map
The Madaba Map is a mosaic floor in a Byzantine Church in Jordan. Dating from about AD 560, it shows the Holy Land in great detail with about 150 significant landmarks. One of the largest and best preserved pieces shows Jerusalem. The southeast corner of Jerusalem has been destroyed, so there is no information about the Temple Mount.

ST STEPHEN'S GATE — GOLDEN GATE — NEA CHURCH — CARDO MAXIMUS — DAMASCUS GATE — HOSPITAL — PALACE OF THE PATRIARCH — CHURCH OF THE HOLY SEPULCHRE — THE FORUM — JAFFA GATE — DECUMANUS — TOWER OF DAVID — CHURCH ON MOUNT ZION

Fountain from the Gate of the Chain (left). The Gate was built by Suleyman the Magnificent in 1537. The trough is probably a coffin from the Crusader age.

A trap door (right) for throwing boiling oil on enemies below. There are many of these around the city walls, particularly above the doors. They were both decorative and useful.

Painting of the inside of the Dome of the Rock. The rock in the foreground is said to be the one on which Abraham prepared to sacrifice his son Isaac. In the Muslim tradition, it is also the place from which Muhammad launched himself heavenward. His footprint is said to be visible on a corner of the rock.

Decoration with an open hand, called a hamsa. They are common on the houses of Arabs and oriental Jews. They are thought to bring good luck and keep away evil.

Pair of panthers from St Stephen's Gate (also known as the Lions Gate). The panther was the heraldic emblem of the Mameluke Sultan Baybars.

Minaret (left) from the Mameluke period. It has the Muslim alam, or half-moon above the dome.

The Damascus Gate (right) leads into the Old City.

Stone eagle, symbol of German imperial power, on the façade of the Lutheran Church of the Redeemer.

HEROD'S GATE

DAMASCUS GATE

ST STEPHEN'S GATE

NEW GATE

CHURCH OF THE HOLY SEPULCHRE

Muslim Quarter

DOME OF THE ROCK

AL-AQSA MOSQUE

Christian Quarter

WESTERN, OR WAILING WALL

JAFFA GATE

CITADEL (TOWER OF DAVID)

Armenian Quarter

Jewish Quarter

DUNG GATE

ZION GATE

The two sides of a Crusader seal. The front shows the Crusader King of Jerusalem, Jean de Brienne, in the 13th century. The back shows the Jaffa Gate, with the Tower of David above it. The Crusaders used the Tower as their castle. The seal also shows the Church of the Holy Sepulchre and the Dome of the Rock.

Jerusalem is also a thriving modern city. The Old City is now surrounded by more recent suburbs. The tower of the YMCA rises in the New City. The YMCA building, dating from 1933, was built by Q.L. Harmon, the same architect who built the Empire State Building in New York. The YMCA building has an amazing mixture of architectural styles, including elements from Romanesque, Moorish, Muslim, Oriental and European traditions.

Emblems of the Imperial Russian Orthodox Society of Palestine are sculpted onto the walls of many 19th-century Russian buildings.

Decorated stone slab, on the wall of St James' Cathedral in the Armenian Quarter.

The Armenians
Armenia has its own quarter in the Old City because when the Kingdom of Armenia disappeared in the 4th century, Armenians adopted Jerusalem as their spiritual capital. Armenia was the first nation to become Christian. Its king converted in AD 303.

Neo-Gothic window from the Anglican Christ Church. It was the first Protestant church in the Holy Land.

The Star of David, with the word Zion in Hebrew letters at the centre. It appears often on 19th-century Jewish doors.

The Taphos (left), Greek for 'tomb', is the emblem of the Greek Orthodox Church. It appears on many Greek Orthodox buildings.

The Dome of the Rock, with the Western Wall in the foreground. The wall is all that remains of the Second Temple area. It is the most holy of all Jewish places.

The Bible and Art

Over the centuries the Bible has inspired painters, sculptors, architects, musicians, poets and other artists to illustrate episodes from it and to give artistic expression to the feelings it enkindles. For hundreds of years, it was practically the only source of inspiration for artists working in the Western world. Today our museums and galleries are filled with examples of paintings and sculptures of religious significance, and many of the greatest works of art are based on events or people from the Bible. It is enough to think of Michelangelo's work in the Sistine Chapel in Rome, Albrecht Dürer's famous woodcuts, or any of the beautiful cathedrals and monasteries in Europe and the rest of the world. Many parts of the Bible itself contain poetry or dramatic writings of the first order. For example, the devotional poetry in Psalms is intensely beautiful.

Stained glass
Many churches have beautiful stained glass windows showing scenes from the Bible. This art form was particularly widespread during the Middle Ages.

Stained glass window from Chartres Cathedral in France, showing events from the parable of the Good Samaritan.

St Basil's Cathedral in Moscow shows a distinctive Eastern influence, typical of the Russian Orthodox Church.

Johann Sebastian Bach (1685–1750) was a German composer and musician. He composed an enormous amount of sacred choral music and three settings of the Passion story.

Religion and music
Music and song have accompanied religious celebrations since earliest times. There are many different types of sacred music. In the Christian tradition, choral music and hymns accompany Mass and other services. For Roman Catholics, Gregorian chant can be sung during Mass.

Michelangelo and the Sistine Chapel
The gigantic frescoes in the Sistine Chapel by the Florentine artist Michelangelo are among the greatest achievements in Western painting. The frescoes on the ceiling, which took the artist four long years to complete, depict events and people in the Old Testament. Twenty years later Michelangelo painted the magnificent *Last Judgement* fresco on the west wall.

Separation of Light and Darkness, *by Michelangelo for the Sistine Ceiling.*

Christian mosaics in the Middle Ages made wide use of gold glass to create shimmering works of art. This mosaic, from the Monreale Cathedral in Palermo, Sicily, shows Adam and Eve with the snake in the Garden of Eden.

The purpose of religious art
In the times when most people were unable to read and write, many pieces of religious art were created to help people to learn the stories and teachings in the Bible.

The mosaic above shows Noah as he releases the animals from the ark after the Flood. It comes from St Mark's Basilica in Venice, Italy, and dates from about AD 1100.

This Turkish painting from 1583 represents The Sacrifice of Isaac. *An angel holding a sacrificial lamb calls out to Abraham just as he is about to kill his son.*

The Birth of Jesus and the Adoration of the Magi is a common theme in Christian art. This is a detail from Fra Angelico's Adoration, *painted in 1451–53 and completed after his death by Fra Filippo Lippi.*

The artist's vision

In the past many artists depicted biblical stories and people in the surroundings of their own time and reflected their own tastes in art. For example, the paintings dating from the Italian Renaissance on this page show European people dressed in Italian clothing of the 14th–16th centuries. This is why Jesus is often shown with blond hair and blue eyes, whereas it seems more likely that he had dark hair and brown eyes.

This famous work by the early Renaissance Italian painter Giotto, shows The Kiss of Judas. *The disciple kisses Jesus the moment before he is pounced on by Roman soldiers. The scene is the first part in the terrible story of the Passion, which leads to Christ's crucifixion.*

This 17th-century painted wooden statue (right) shows Christ after he has risen from the dead as he meets Mary Magdalene.

The Crucifixion, *by Italian Renaissance painter Vincenzo Foppa. The Crucifixion is of fundamental importance to Christian belief; Christ's death on the cross has been represented so many times that it has become a symbol for the religion itself.*

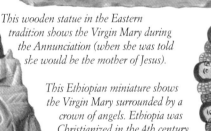

This wooden statue in the Eastern tradition shows the Virgin Mary during the Annunciation (when she was told she would be the mother of Jesus).

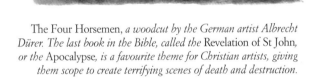

This Ethiopian miniature shows the Virgin Mary surrounded by a crown of angels. Ethiopia was Christianized in the 4th century AD. It resisted conquest by Muslim Arabs in the 7th century. There is still a large Christian population in Ethiopia today.

The Four Horsemen, *a woodcut by the German artist Albrecht Dürer. The last book in the Bible, called the* Revelation of St John, *or the* Apocalypse, *is a favourite theme for Christian artists, giving them scope to create terrifying scenes of death and destruction.*

Symbols

Symbols represent or stand for a person, group or idea. The Star of David or the menorah are common Jewish symbols, while the cross is widely used to represent Christianity.

The cross is a symbol of Christ's crucifixion and of Christianity in general. In early Christian art the fish was a symbol of Christ. The Greek word for fish is ichthys; these letters represent Iesous Christos theou hyios soter *(Jesus Christ, Son of God, the Saviour).*

The lamb was a sacrificial animal for the Hebrews. The early Christians adopted it as a symbol of Christ's sacrifice; for this reason it is often shown together with a cross.

Medieval sculpture

This detail from a medieval church in Provence, France, shows Christ with his hand raised in benediction. He is surrounded by symbolic representations of Matthew, Mark, Luke and John.

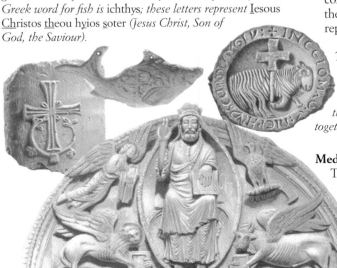

Israel and the Middle East

Today the Bible Lands are divided among the modern Arab states of the Middle East and the Jewish state of Israel. Constant persecution during the 19th century made some Jews, particularly in Russia, believe that they would never be fully accepted in Europe. A small group formed the Zionist movement with the aim of founding a Jewish homeland in Palestine. With the support of the Zionists, a steady trickle of migrants moved to Palestine. By the time the First World War broke out in 1914 there were about 90,000 Jews settled in Palestine. In the years leading up to the Second World War, many more Jews arrived from Europe, especially when the German Nazi régime began to persecute and slaughter Jews. In 1947 a United Nations plan was to divide Palestine into a Jewish area and a Palestinian area. The Jews agreed, but the Arab inhabitants of Palestine, who had bitterly opposed Jewish settlement from the start, were outraged. War broke out immediately. The State of Israel was proclaimed on May 14, 1948, although the war continued until the Israelis won in 1949. Since then Arabs and Israelis have fought several wars over Israel's right to exist and the Palestinian right to a homeland. By the late 1990s, despite some progress with peace treaties, no solution to the problem had been found.

David Ben-Gurion, first Prime Minister of Israel in 1948.

Woman waving the Zionist flag. The ancient homeland of the Jews is known in Hebrew as Eretz Israel (Land of Israel).

Three leaders of the Zionist movement. From left: Max Nordau, Theodor Herzl and Prof. Mandelstamm. The scenes below the portraits show the two Zionist ideals of settling in Israel – land to farm on and proximity to the Western Wall in Jerusalem.

In Nazi areas Jews were forced to wear a yellow star sewn on to their clothing.

Nazi Germany

Adolf Hitler's fascist dictatorship came to power in Germany in 1933. As Nazi power spread, more and more Jews were persecuted. Most of those who did not escape were exterminated. Six million Jews from all over Europe died in Nazi concentration camps during the war. Many of those who escaped or who survived the death camps went to Israel.

The revival of the Hebrew language

As the Zionist dream of returning to Palestine took shape, it was decided that a new language was needed to unite the settlers as a nation. Rejecting the Eastern European Yiddish as the language of exile, they chose to revive ancient Hebrew. This was not an easy task. Hebrew was then a 'dead' language, in the sense that it had not been spoken (except in religious rituals) for about 1,700 years. It existed as a written language, in the Torah and other religious and literary texts. But the modern world required many new words and expressions which had to be borrowed from other languages. Incredibly, it worked and modern Hebrew, now spoken by more than five million people, is fast becoming the international language of the Jewish people both in Israel and abroad.

Zionist settlers spread out over the territory, farming the dry land to increase production. Many farms were organized as kibbutzim, with several family groups living together and sharing the work and profits. One of the major points of conflict, which has hindered the peace process between Palestinians and Israelis, has been the refusal of Jewish settlers to move out of the areas occupied by Israel after the Six-Day War in 1967, including the West Bank, the Gaza Strip and the Golan Heights.

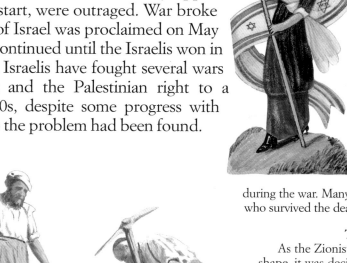

Immigration today

Not all Jews live in Israel. Of the estimated 13 million Jewish people in the world today, about one-third are Israeli citizens. However, there is strong support among many non-Israeli Jews for the State of Israel. They back Israel financially, morally and politically. Since the late 1980s many new immigrants have come from Russia.

American Zionist movement poster (left).

Jewish National Fund poster from the 1930s in Hebrew, Yiddish and Polish saying 'Let us redeem the (Jezreel) Valley' (in Israel) (right).

Into the future

In 1998 Israel celebrated its 50th birthday. Although it seems to have solved its most basic problem of simply surviving, it is still a young nation with many questions to resolve. Beyond the continuing search for peace with neighbouring countries and the Palestinian question, Israel must also face up to many divisions within itself. There is a division between its orthodox and secular (non religious) citizens, and another division between its Ashkenazim (European Jews) and Sephardim (Jews from Arab countries) citizens. Although they form the majority of the population, the Sephardim often feel that they have been treated as second-class citizens. Absorbing the continual flow of immigrants is also a challenge.

The search for peace

Israel and the Arab nations have fought four full-scale wars since 1948. Innumerable acts of terrorism by both sides have cost many more lives. About 300,000 Palestinians fled to neighbouring countries when Israel was formed. Denied citizenship in Arab countries, they have been forced to live in refugee camps. Led by Yasser Arafat and the Palestinian Liberation Organization (PLO) Palestinians sought recognition and a homeland at first by war and acts of terrorism. In 1989 the PLO recognized Israel's right to exist. Since then it has adopted the policy of accepting separate Israeli and Palestinian states. Palestine now has limited self-government in the Gaza Strip and the West Bank. In the late 1990s a permanent peace accord was being negotiated but the outcome was by no means assured.

King Hussein of Jordan (below). A peace treaty was signed with Jordan in 1994.

Hafiz el-Assad, president and dictator of Syria from 1970. Syria has always violently opposed Israel's existence and is still, along with Lebanon, officially at war with the Jewish nation.

Islamic fundamentalism in Arab countries has led some extreme groups and governments to call for a Holy War against non-Islamic peoples. Iran under the ayatollahs has strongly opposed Israel and the entire Western world, although in the late 1990s it became more tolerant.

Jimmy Carter, President of the United States, with Egypt's Anwar Sadat and Israel's Menachem Begin celebrate the peace agreement reached between the two countries in 1979. Sadat was assassinated by Arab extremists in 1981.

Lethal F-15 fighter planes above the Dome of the Rock. This picture is typical of daily life in Israel, which is still officially at war with some neighbouring Arab states.

Pope John Paul II meets the chief Rabbi in Rome, Elio Toaff. Vatican diplomats have been trying to arrange a papal visit to the Holy Land for years.

President Clinton with Palestinian leader Yasser Arafat (right) and Israel's Prime Minister Yitzhak Rabin (left) as they agree to a peace settlement in 1993. They agreed that there would be self-governing Palestinian areas within the occupied territories. Both Arab and Jewish extremists protested. Rabin was assassinated by an extremist Jew in 1995.

Index